Gender, Race, and Office Holding in the United States

Over the last several decades, the number of women elected to higher office in the United States has grown substantially. However, when the electoral gains of women are considered on a state-by-state basis, there are observable variations in the rate by state at which women are elected to state legislative office. Scholars have noted an additional variation in women office holders: that women of color serve at higher rates than do white women.

Becki Scola's book provides an explanation for these two interrelated puzzles on electoral gender gaps. She examines the factors surrounding the uneven proportional distribution of female legislators and then explores why gender appears to be an advantage for women of color office holders. Through an examination of the divergent state-level institutional and environmental conditions, Scola maps out the factors that contribute to more, or less, female legislative service and how race/ethnicity intersects with these conditions. She reveals that the common conceptions and theories that help us understand women's office holding in general do not equally apply to both white women and women of color's legislative service.

The first book-length study to analyze how race informs gender in terms of patterns of office holding, *Gender, Race, and Office Holding in the United States* provides insight into both underrepresentation in general as well as the underlying dynamics of representation within specific groups of women.

Becki Scola is an Assistant Professor at Saint Joseph's University. Her research interests include American institutions, gender politics, race/ethnic politics, and social justice policy. She has published in *State Politics & Policy Quarterly*, *Journal of Women, Politics & Policy*, and *Politics & Gender*, and she is currently completing a project that examines antihunger advocacy at the intersection of gender and race/ethnicity in Philadelphia, as well as a study that examines women's path to office in Pennsylvania.

Routledge Research in American Politics and Governance

1 **Lobbying the New President**
Interests in Transition
Heath Brown

2 **Religion, Race, and Barack Obama's New Democratic Pluralism**
Gastón Espinosa

3 **Direct Democracy in the United States**
Petitioners as a Reflection of Society
Edited by Shauna Reilly and Ryan M. Yonk

4 **American Exceptionalism in the Age of Obama**
Stephen Brooks

5 **"An Empire of Ideals"**
The Chimeric Imagination of Ronald Reagan
Justin D. Garrison

6 **Resisting Injustice and the Feminist Ethics of Care in the Age of Obama**
"Suddenly, . . . All the Truth Was Coming Out"
David A.J. Richards

7 **Interfaith Advocacy**
The Role of Religious Coalitions in the Political Process
Katherine E. Knutson

8 **Social Contract Theory in American Jurisprudence**
Too Much Liberty and Too Much Authority
Thomas R. Pope

9 **Voting and Migration Patterns in the U.S.**
George Hawley

10 **Democracy, Intelligent Design, and Evolution**
Science for Citizenship
Susan P. Liebell

11 **Inventive Politicians and Ethnic Ascent in American Politics**
The Uphill Elections of Italians and Mexicans to the U.S. Congress
Miriam Jiménez

12 **Competitive Elections and Democracy in America**
The Good, the Bad, and the Ugly
Heather K. Evans

13 **Gender, Race, and Office Holding in the United States**
Representation at the Intersections
Becki Scola

Gender, Race, and Office Holding in the United States
Representation at the Intersections

Becki Scola

First published 2014
by Routledge
711 Third Avenue, New York, NY 10017

and by Routledge
2 Park Square, Milton Park, Abingdon, Oxfordshire OX14 4RN

Routledge is an imprint of the Taylor and Francis Group, an informa business

First issued in paperback 2015

© 2014 Taylor & Francis

The right of Becki Scola to be identified as author of this work has been asserted by her in accordance with sections 77 and 78 of the Copyright, Designs and Patents Act 1988.

All rights reserved. No part of this book may be reprinted or reproduced or utilized in any form or by any electronic, mechanical, or other means, now known or hereafter invented, including photocopying and recording, or in any information storage or retrieval system, without permission in writing from the publishers.

Trademark Notice: Product or corporate names may be trademarks or registered trademarks, and are used only for identification and explanation without intent to infringe.

Library of Congress Cataloging-in-Publication Data
Scola, Becki.
  Gender, race, and office holding in the United States : representation at the intersections / by Becki Scola.
      pages cm. — (Routledge research in American politics and governance ; 13)
  1. Women legislators—United States—States. 2. Minority legislators—United States—States. 3. Legislative bodies—United States—States. 4. Representative government and representation—United States—States. 5. Women—Political activity—United States—States. 6. Political culture—United States—States. I. Title.
  HQ1391.U5S36 2013
  320.082—dc23
  2013030569

ISBN 978-0-415-85434-4 (hbk)
ISBN 978-1-138-12470-7 (pbk)
ISBN 978-0-203-74408-6 (ebk)

Typeset in Sabon
by Apex CoVantage, LLC

To Madalyn, Devon, and Julian for all of their patience, understanding, and unconditional love and support.

Contents

List of Figures and Tables xi
Acknowledgments xiii

1 Introduction: The Puzzle of Legislative Service by Women of Color 1

2 Geographical Variation, the Gender Gap, and Intersecting Theories of Representation 27

3 Mapping the Terrain: Descriptive Representation at the Intersection of Gender and Race/Ethnicity 63

4 Geographical Variation at the Intersection 101

5 Gender Gaps at the Intersection 123

6 Conclusion: Representation at the Intersections 133

References 149
Index 163

Figures and Tables

Figures

1.1 Women Legislators as a Percentage of Their Respective Racial/Ethnic Group, 2010   12

3.1 Percentage of State Legislative Office Holding for Women, White Women, and Women of Color, 1990–2010   75

3.2 Percentage of State Legislative Office Holding for Legislators of Color, Men of Color, and Women of Color, 1990–2010   79

Tables

1.1 Percentage of Women, White Women, and Women of Color in State Legislature by State, 2010   9

1.2 Aggregate Percentage Summary of the Variation in State Legislative Office Holding for Various Groups, 2010   11

1.3 Women of Color Legislators and White Women Legislators as a Percentage of Their Racial/Ethnic Group by State, 2010   13

2.1 Intersectional Typology of Representation at the State Level: Will a State have Higher Percentages of Women, White Women, and Women of Color Legislators?   48

3.1 State Rankings for Women's Legislative Representation, Pooled Percentages by Group, 1990–2010   69

3.2 State Rankings for Legislators of Color Representation, Pooled Percentages by Group, 1990–2010   72

xii *Figures and Tables*

3.3	Pooled Percentage and Increase/Decrease of Women in State Legislatures, by Group and State, 1990–2010	76
3.4	Pooled Percentage and Increase/Decrease of Legislators of Color in State Legislatures by Group and State, 1990–2010	81
3.5	Pooled Percentage and Increase/Decrease in the Gender Gap in State Legislatures by Group and State, 1990–2010	86
3.6	State Rankings for Gender Gap, Pooled Percentages by Group, 1990–2010	90
3.7	State Rankings for Increase/Decrease in Gender Gaps, Pooled Percentages by Group, 1990–2010	94
4.1	Unstandardized Regression Coefficients (and Standard Errors) for the Percent of Women, White Women, and Women of Color in State Legislatures	107
4.2	Unstandardized Regression Coefficients (and Standard Errors) for the Percentage of Legislators of Color, Men of Color, and Women of Color in State Legislatures	112
4.3	Modified Typology: Predictors of Descriptive Representation at the State Level	116
5.1	Unstandardized Regression Coefficients (and Standard Errors) for the White and Legislator of Color Gender Gap in State Legislatures	125
5.2	Combined Gender Gap and Geographical Variation Typology: Predictors of Women's State Level Descriptive Representation	130

Acknowledgments

This project would not have been possible without much-needed financial support from the University of California, Irvine's Department of Political Science and the School of Social Sciences, as well as St. Joseph's University's Office of the Provost. I extend my appreciation to these institutions for their generosity with summer research grants and funding.

I would like to extend my sincerest appreciation to all of the colleagues who provided feedback, support, and encouragement throughout this entire process. First, to Mark Petracca and Carole Uhlaner, whose attention, expertise, and guidance were always on target and sincerely respected. Mark graciously supplied steadfast dedication and confidence in my work, no matter where I was, both in terms of my mental frame of mind or my physical location. His door (and e-mail) was forever open, he was generous with his time, and his counsel was continuously inspirational. The many hours I spent in Carole's office are ones I will always remember. Carole never tired of talking (and explaining) all things statistical and gently prodded me to take my skills to the next level. She continues to be a source of motivation and always provides me with a challenge when I need one.

I would also like to thank Louis DeSipio for his calm reassurance whenever I had moments of doubt and my mind felt chaotic. Louis was readily available, via phone or e-mail, with pragmatic advice and much needed clarity. Matthew Beckmann encouraged me to think more theoretically about the empirical puzzles that are the foundation of this manuscript. Matt's ideas and vision structured my research findings in a way that I could have never done on my own.

Both Lisa Baglione and Kazuya Fukuoka provided helpful comments and suggestions on portions of the manuscript. And, Lisa granted me the leeway to prioritize this project above all else, departmental or otherwise. I could not have completed this process without her considerate support and thoughtfulness.

This project may not ever have turned into a book without Susan Liebell's encouragement to "just submit a proposal and see what happens." Susan was there to remind me to see the forest for the trees, especially when I veered off course. The camaraderie and advice she provided kept me sane and focused. Here's to many more coffee and chocolate breaks!

I owe a great deal to Lindsey Lupo. Lindsey's suggestion to have biweekly phone meetings dug me out of the hole of procrastination in which I was stuck. I am not sure if I would have ever finished many parts of this project if it were not for her voice at the end of the line every few weeks. Thank you, Lindsey. I am so grateful for your friendship and advice. I look forward to our future collaborations!

So many undergraduates were an integral part of this process, and I thank all of them. Without their willingness and eagerness to be a part of this research, I would have been much more overwhelmed. I am particularly indebted to Kristen Harper, whose dedicated research assistance is evident in every single page of this book. I could not have finished this manuscript without her careful editing, suggestions, and expertise. Kristen, I am forever indebted to you!

Finally, I am especially grateful to my children, Madalyn, Devon, and Julian, who deserve the most appreciation. For every day that they waited patiently for an end to the work day, for every time they encouraged me keep going, for the countless situations that they extended their understanding, I thank you. This goal has been for you as much as it has been for me. I hope that all three of you realize your own aspirations, whatever they may be.

1 Introduction
The Puzzle of Legislative Service by Women of Color

When they told us 1992 was the year of the woman, we didn't realize it was going to be just one year.
—Marie Wilson, White House Project, 2006

The election cycle of 2012 prompted political pundits, scholars, and the media to declare the potentiality of another "Year of the Woman," much like the one we had witnessed twenty years earlier. More women were running and, as the adage goes, when women run, they win. Indeed, 2012 did not disappoint. We saw an increase in women's Congressional office holding, and there was plenty of press coverage about the new cohort of female representatives. At the state level, however, we witnessed only modest increases, and these gains were not evenly distributed across the fifty state legislatures—some states realized increases in women's representation, while other states recorded losses.

Assessing the gender gap in office holding is not a new question. Women and politics scholars have investigated the phenomenon for more than four decades now at the local, state, national, and international level. We know quite a bit about the differences between male and female elected officials along with myriad explanations for why there are fewer women than men in our legislative institutions. Everything from campaign contexts to fund-raising to voter attitudes to institutional rules and structures helps explain the gender gap in office holding. In other words, the differences between men and women in politics are a well-researched, well-documented area of intellectual inquiry. What is also a fairly well-examined question is why we see a variation in female office holding

2 Gender, Race, and Office Holding in the United States

across the fifty U.S. states. It has been asked and answered by several scholars of women and politics, resulting in variety of compelling conclusions including psychosociological orientations among men and women, state-level contextual environments, and the institutional-level rules of the game.

What has not been asked and answered sufficiently is the question, Does what we "know" about women in politics apply equally to *all* women? The intuitive answer to this question is no, and in the United States, we have some evidence to support that there are differences regarding political party affiliation, political party recruitment, and where Republican and Democratic women are more or less likely to serve at the state level.[1] Political party affiliation, then, assists us in developing a partial understanding of why we see a variation in women's office holding across the state legislative institutions.

However, other important dimensions of difference among women have not been systematically studied in relation to the gender gap in office holding. For example, in the United States, race/ethnicity is arguably one of those significant dimensions. We have very little to guide our understanding of how the race/ethnicity of the female office holder corresponds to the conventional wisdom about where female state legislators serve. This is still an open question, and one worth answering because the gender gap in state legislative office holding is smaller for legislators of color than it is for white legislators. To say it another way, in 2010, of all state legislators of color, 34.9% were women; of all white legislators, 22.5% were women.[2] Why do women of color serve at relatively higher rates than their white female counterparts? What explains the smaller gender gap in state legislative office holding among legislators of color?

This book offers an empirical investigation of female office holding at the intersection of gender and race/ethnicity and argues that an intersectional approach complicates our understanding of where women are more or less likely to serve. I find that the conventional wisdom does not apply equally to all women office holders if we take the race/ethnicity of the legislator into account. The mix of demographic, contextual, and institutional variables most commonly cited as explanations for the geographical variation of female legislators provide less leverage when applied to different racial/ethnic groups of women. Why? That is the first puzzle under investigation.

The second, but related, question takes this one step further and examines the smaller racial/ethnic gender gap in office holding. Why do women of color, when considered as a proportion of their respective racial/ethnic groups, serve at higher rates than their white female counterparts? My analysis reveals that the theories and conceptions that guide our knowledge about female office holding are distinctly different for white women and women of color legislators.

A few new questions emerge if the women of color are placed at the center of analysis. If women of color serve at relatively higher rates than do their white female counterparts, is it because they encounter a different set of opportunities or face a different set of barriers? Are they more likely to run for office? If we know, for instance, that (1) women face institutional barriers that impede their candidacies and (2) women are less ambitious in terms of running for office, then we might theorize that women of color face fewer institutional barriers and are more ambitious than white women.[3] On the flip side, we might expect just the opposite to occur. Women of color may face what has been called a "double disadvantage"—they are both women and of color.[4] Purportedly, they would face more significant institutional barriers than would white women and should be less politically ambitious. Yet, it appears that neither of these propositions maps very well on to the empirical evidence.

To be sure, there is a burgeoning literature that investigates women of color officeholders at the state level.[5] These studies seek to illuminate the experiences and decisions of women of color, an important area of inquiry that has received very little attention.[6] The goal is to examine the legislative behavior of women of color and how they view their role as a legislator, as well as their goals, agendas, and policy perspectives. Within this collection of studies are several that analyze the differences between men and women of color and how gender has an impact on legislative behavior—in other words, a *gendered* analysis of *race/ethnicity*. What we see less of in the women and politics literature is a *racial/ethnic* analysis of *gender*.

The intent of this book is to provide just that: a racial/ethnic analysis of gender and office holding, guided by intersectional theory, utilizing the smaller racial/ethnic gender gap as the empirical test. It is the first book-length study to investigate how the race/ethnicity of a female state legislator informs our comprehension of women's elective service across the states. I seek to uncover an explanation for the smaller racial gender gap, identify the factors that might make the electoral environment more favorable for women of color than for white women, and highlight the core contexts and structures that are different for white women and women of color.

An intersectional analysis provides a more nuanced theory of women's office holding and amends the conventional approaches used to explain the gender gap in legislative service. I contend that the institutional structures and individual processes most commonly cited to account for women's low levels of legislative service do not account for the variation in state-level office holding by women of color or the smaller racial/ethnic gender gap in office holding. What we "know" about the gender gap in office holding at the state level, the conventional wisdom, primarily applies to white female state legislators, and I demonstrate how and where this wisdom does not pertain to women of color state legislators. This book attempts to build on the knowledge within the women and politics literature by offering an assessment of the geographical variation in office holding by women of color as well as their proportionally smaller gender gap in legislative service at the state level compared to white women legislators.

REPRESENTATION AT THE STATE LEVEL

Why should we even care about the demographic composition of our state legislatures? The unequal distribution and attainment of formal political power to certain groups has been a mainstay throughout U.S. history.[7] Gender and race are two such identities that have organized U.S. politics, producing advantages for white men and disadvantages to others. Both women and minorities are historically disadvantaged groups within American politics: they have experienced legal, systematic exclusion from formal political processes, such as voting, and avenues of representation, such as holding office. And, although women and minorities are no longer legally excluded from formal political arenas such as voting and office holding, both groups have yet to realize proportional representation in comparison to their population within our legislative institutions.

Representation is the core of democratic theory, because it imparts legitimacy for our system of government and accountability for those that are serving as representatives. But defining exactly what "representation" is and what it looks like can be difficult. Hanna Pitkin defines representation as "the making present of something which is nevertheless not literally present."[8] Pitkin differentiates between descriptive and substantive representation as a way to mitigate the competing interests a representative might face. Descriptive representation "depends on the representative's characteristics, on what he *is* or is *like*, on being something rather than doing something. The representative does not act for others; he 'stands for' them, by virtue of a correspondence or connection between them, a resemblance or reflection."[9]

Although descriptive representation is about "standing for" the population, substantive representation, Pitkin argues, is "acting for" the population.[10] In the instance of political choices, she states, "We need [substantive] representation precisely where we are not content to leave matters to the expert; we can have substantive representation only where interest is involved, that is, where decisions are not merely arbitrary choices."[11] The question then becomes whether one can get "substantive" representation in an institution that is not "descriptive." For Pitkin, that is still an open question. Her main concern is with interests and the process and less so with the outcome—it is a representative institution if the process is democratic.[12]

Pitkin notes that representative government should be defined as long-term, systematic arrangements that impart regular, systematic responsiveness. She contends that a representative government has to demonstrate that its subjects have control over what it does. In other words, *the people* act through their government and are not merely passive recipients of its actions. The *governed* must be capable of action and judgment, capable of initiating government activity so that the government can be conceived as responding to them.

When people do not feel as if they are a part of these institutions, they are less engaged in the political process. Consequently, they feel less politically efficacious, they participate less in politics, and they are less informed about the political process—government becomes less legitimate for them. Indeed, studies show that women and minorities participate in fewer political acts and have less information and interest in politics compared to white men.[13] Because white men are overrepresented in our governing institutions, one might reason that their heightened representation leads to their higher levels of participation and efficacy. The converse, then, would be true for women and minorities, for whom the lack of descriptive representation would lead to depressed participation.

In fact, research does document an increase in registration, voting, participation, information, and interest among women and minorities when they are represented by someone who looks like them.[14] Furthermore, when gender is cued in elections in the form of a female candidate or in strategies focusing on women's issues in the campaign, women vote for women.[15] Racial and ethnic minorities are also mobilized when a minority candidate is on the ticket as well as when a minority is in office.[16] Matson and Fine find that both gender and ethnicity serve as voting cues under certain circumstances, and Stout and Tate contend that "higher levels of efficacy are *the result* of descriptive representation, rather than simply being correlated with descriptive representation."[17]

Thus, women and minorities are less engaged politically at the individual level. But having a female or a minority representative alleviates this disengagement at the mass level. Descriptive representation of historically underrepresented groups, then, mobilizes these groups to become active in the political process, to be more interested in politics, and to seek more political information, thereby enhancing the democratic process as a whole. To say it another way, if what Pitkin refers to as the "process" of government looks descriptively like certain groups, namely, women and minorities, then those groups are more engaged in politics, which means that they feel as if the system is "responding to them."

Of course, like Pitkin, some maintain that descriptive representation is not enough, and that what really matters is substantive representation, which may or may not be part and parcel of descriptive representation. What we find, however, is that women and minority legislators promote and follow a legislative agenda that corresponds to the differences in public opinion we see at the mass level. Women representatives are more likely than are men to prioritize, promote, introduce, and pass legislation that specifically attends to the social welfare of women, families, and children.[18] Similarly, the evidence on legislators of color suggests that the agenda of minority legislators specifically attends to minority interests.[19]

In short, the literature on the link between representation and political participation has established that (1) descriptive representation mobilizes participation among historically underrepresented groups and (2) women and minority legislators promote an agenda that differs from their white male counterparts. Because our government is a system based on representing divergent collective interests, then it is imperative that our governing institutions actually represent the entirety of public interests and identities. When certain groups, such as gender and racial/ethnic groups, are not represented descriptively or substantively, then we should be skeptical of the representational capacity of our institutions. In other words, if particular voices are not present at the table of legislative assemblies, namely, the voices that have divergent views from those that are currently holding office, then we are missing critical points of view from which our laws are constructed. If the preceding theoretical discussion on representation is true, then our legislative institutions are doing poorly in terms of women and minorities. Because we know that women and minorities are greatly underrepresented in our democratic institutions, we need to know how our institutional and social structures support or impede the potential for their representation.

State legislatures are an ideal place to study this unrealized representation. Ford and Dolan suggest two reasons as to why research on women in state legislatures is important.[20] The first is practicality: unlike Congress, there are a large number of women in state legislatures, which lends itself to systematic study. Second, Ford and Dolan state that most "issues of direct concern to women are decided at the state level."[21] In other words, policies that have a significant impact on the daily lives of women are most likely to occur at the state level.[22] Of course, states are not equal in a variety of ways, which is exactly why they are primed for comparative analysis while still being able to hold the context of the nation constant.[23] Ostrander and Lien contend that focusing on the congressional level "does not allow scholars to test whether alternative electoral systems might enhance the elections of racial and gender minorities to governing bodies."[24] In other words, there are fifty legislative contexts across which we can study the patterns of representation among groups of women.

GEOGRAPHICAL VARIATION, THE GENDER GAP, AND INTERSECTIONALITY

To be sure, women have made substantial gains in elective office in the United States during the past few decades. In 1975, women constituted 8% of state legislators, and by 2010, 24.2% of all state legislators were women.[25] Despite these gains, women, especially women of color,[26] are greatly underrepresented in state legislatures in comparison to their population proportions.[27]

What is more is that women's office holding is not uniform across the country. Some states approach (or have approached) parity whereas others are struggling to get out of the single digits. In short, geographically, there is a variation in the rate of office holding across the fifty states for women. Table 1.1 illustrates the cross-sectional variation we see for female office holding for 2010 for (1) all women, (2) white women, and (3) women of color. The percentage of women in state legislatures ranged from a low of 10.0% in South Carolina to a high

Table 1.1 Percentage of Women, White Women, and Women of Color in State Legislature by State, 2010

State	Total in Leg	Women	White Women	Women of Color
Alabama	140	12.9%	5.7%	7.1%
Alaska	60	21.7%	20.0%	1.7%
Arizona	90	32.2%	22.2%	10.0%
Arkansas	135	23.0%	19.3%	3.7%
California	120	26.7%	14.2%	12.5%
Colorado	100	38.0%	34.0%	4.0%
Connecticut	187	32.1%	28.9%	3.2%
Delaware	62	25.8%	22.6%	3.2%
Florida	160	23.8%	15.6%	8.1%
Georgia	236	19.5%	12.3%	7.2%
Hawaii	76	32.9%	7.9%	25.0%
Idaho	105	25.7%	24.8%	1.0%
Illinois	177	28.2%	17.5%	10.7%
Indiana	150	21.3%	18.0%	3.3%
Iowa	150	23.3%	20.7%	2.7%
Kansas	165	30.3%	26.7%	3.6%
Kentucky	138	15.9%	15.9%	0.0%
Louisiana	144	16.0%	7.6%	8.3%
Maine	186	29.0%	29.0%	0.0%
Maryland	188	31.4%	18.1%	13.3%
Massachusetts	200	25.5%	23.0%	2.5%
Michigan	148	25.0%	21.6%	3.4%
Minnesota	201	34.8%	33.8%	1.0%
Mississippi	174	14.4%	6.9%	7.5%
Missouri	197	22.3%	17.3%	5.1%
Montana	150	26.0%	22.7%	3.3%
Nebraska	49	20.4%	16.3%	4.1%
Nevada	63	31.7%	30.2%	1.6%
New Hampshire	424	36.8%	35.6%	1.2%
New Jersey	120	28.3%	16.7%	11.7%

(Continued)

Table 1.1 (Continued)

State	Total in Leg	Women	White Women	Women of Color
New Mexico	112	30.4%	14.3%	16.1%
New York	212	24.1%	17.0%	7.1%
North Carolina	170	25.9%	19.4%	6.5%
North Dakota	141	16.3%	16.3%	0.0%
Ohio	132	22.0%	15.9%	6.1%
Oklahoma	149	11.4%	8.7%	2.7%
Oregon	90	28.9%	26.7%	2.2%
Pennsylvania	253	15.4%	12.6%	2.8%
Rhode Island	113	22.1%	19.5%	2.7%
South Carolina	170	10.0%	6.5%	3.5%
South Dakota	105	20.0%	20.0%	0.0%
Tennessee	132	18.9%	10.6%	8.3%
Texas	181	23.8%	12.2%	11.6%
Utah	104	22.1%	20.2%	1.9%
Vermont	180	37.2%	36.7%	0.6%
Virginia	140	19.3%	12.1%	7.1%
Washington	147	32.7%	28.6%	4.1%
West Virginia	134	16.4%	14.9%	1.5%
Wisconsin	132	22.0%	18.9%	3.0%
Wyoming	90	16.7%	16.7%	0.0%

of 38% in Colorado. White women's service ranged from a low of 5.7% in Alabama to a high of 36.7% in Vermont. There were no women of color serving in Kentucky, Maine, North Dakota, South Dakota, or Wyoming. But, in Hawaii, women of color make up 25.0% of state legislators.[28]

Table 1.2 summarizes this variation by listing the high and low percentages for women, white women, and women of color legislators for 2010, comparing this the range in office holding for legislators of color and men of color. The geographical variation in office holding is much higher for legislators of color when compared to women legislators.

Table 1.2 Aggregate Percentage Summary of the Variation in State Legislative Office Holding for Various Groups, 2010

Year 2010	Women	Legislators of Color	White Women	Women of Color	Men of Color
High	38.0%	85.5%	36.7%	25.0%	60.5%
Low	10.0%	0.6%	5.7%	0.0%	0.0%

Hawaii is comprised of the highest percentage of legislators of color at 85.5%, while Vermont rings in as the lowest at 0.6%. No men of color served in Nebraska or Vermont legislatures, but Hawaii, again, at 60.5% men of color legislators, took the top spot.[29]

As stated earlier, women of color, as a proportion of their racial/ethnic groups, serve at higher rates than do white women as a percentage of whites. In other words, the gender gap in office holding is smaller for women of color. This is a counterintuitive trend, because whereas women in general may have a disadvantage regarding office holding, previous literature posited that women of color may experience a "double disadvantage" in terms of electoral service.[30] According to Moncrief, Thompson, and Shuhmann, "the 'double-disadvantage' hypothesis . . . suggests that because of both their race and gender, black women will find it especially difficult to compete successfully in electoral politics in the United States."[31] Even so, almost all of the studies on this topic have discounted the double disadvantage and, instead, have suggested that women of color may experience a double *advantage*.

Indeed, several scholars have noted that women of color serve at higher rates than do white women.[32] So, although women of color still do not reflect their proportion of the population, they *do* serve at higher levels than white women as a proportion of their respective racial/ethnic group. Furthermore, not all racial/ethnic groups of women serve at the same rate. Figure 1.1 illustrates the proportional racial/ethnic rate of elective service at the state legislative level for white women, black women, Latinas, Asian American women and Native American women for the year 2010.

12　Gender, Race, and Office Holding in the United States

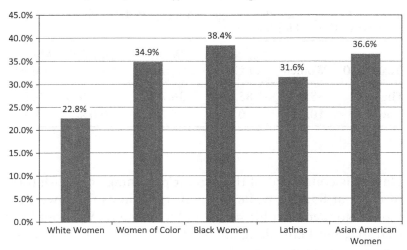

Figure 1.1　Women Legislators as a Percentage of Their Respective Racial/Ethnic Group, 2010

In 2010, white women constituted 22.8% of all white legislators, whereas women of color composed 34.9% of all legislators of color. Black female legislators had the highest rates of proportional representation at 38.4% of all black legislators, followed closely by Asian American women at 36.6% of all Asian American state legislators. Latinas represented 31.6% of all Latino office holders at the state level. This demonstrates, in broad strokes, that the gender gap in office holding is smaller for legislators of color when compared to white legislators.

Table 1.3 breaks this down by state and reports the percentages for both women of color and white women as a percentage of their respective racial/ethnic group for the year 2010, as well as the difference in the proportion, with the negative numbers indicating where women of color legislators are serving at higher proportional rates than white women.

One of the first things to note is that there is geographical variation in both women of color and white women's proportional representation. As a percentage of all legislators of color, the rates of proportional representation by women of color range from a low of 0.0% to a high of 100.0%. For example, they represent the entire delegation in Nebraska

Table 1.3 Women of Color Legislators and White Women Legislators as a Percentage of Their Racial/Ethnic Group by State, 2010

State	Total in Legislature	Women of Color as a Percentage of Legislators of Color	White Women as a Percentage of White Legislators	Difference in Proportional Representation
Alabama	140	29.4%	7.5%	−21.9%
Alaska	60	11.1%	23.5%	12.4%
Arizona	90	47.4%	28.2%	−19.2%
Arkansas	135	35.7%	21.5%	−14.2%
California	120	38.5%	21.0%	−17.5%
Colorado	100	44.4%	37.4%	−7.1%
Connecticut	187	25.0%	33.1%	8.1%
Delaware	62	33.3%	25.0%	−8.3%
Florida	160	31.0%	21.2%	−9.8%
Georgia	236	28.8%	16.4%	−12.4%
Hawaii	76	29.2%	54.5%	25.3%
Idaho	105	50.0%	25.2%	−24.8%
Illinois	177	46.3%	22.8%	−23.5%
Indiana	150	41.7%	19.6%	−22.1%
Iowa	150	57.1%	21.7%	−35.5%
Kansas	165	60.0%	28.4%	−31.6%
Kentucky	138	0.0%	16.9%	16.9%
Louisiana	144	41.4%	9.6%	−31.8%
Maine	186	0.0%	29.3%	29.3%
Maryland	188	51.0%	24.5%	−26.6%
Massachusetts	200	50.0%	24.2%	−25.8%
Michigan	148	16.7%	27.1%	10.5%
Minnesota	201	25.0%	35.2%	10.2%
Mississippi	174	26.0%	9.7%	−16.3%
Missouri	197	50.0%	19.2%	−30.8%
Montana	150	50.0%	24.3%	−25.7%

(Continued)

Table 1.3 (Continued)

State	Total in Legislature	Women of Color as a Percentage of Legislators of Color	White Women as a Percentage of White Legislators	Difference in Proportional Representation
Nebraska	49	100.0%	17.0%	−83.0%
Nevada	63	8.3%	37.3%	28.9%
New Hampshire	424	71.4%	36.2%	−35.2%
New Jersey	120	60.9%	20.6%	−40.3%
New Mexico	112	31.6%	29.1%	−2.5%
New York	212	29.4%	22.4%	−7.1%
North Carolina	170	34.4%	23.9%	−10.5%
North Dakota	141	0.0%	16.5%	16.5%
Ohio	132	47.1%	18.3%	−28.8%
Oklahoma	149	13.8%	10.8%	−3.0%
Oregon	90	66.7%	27.6%	−39.1%
Pennsylvania	253	25.9%	14.2%	−11.8%
Rhode Island	113	42.9%	20.8%	−22.1%
South Carolina	170	15.4%	8.4%	−7.0%
South Dakota	105	0.0%	20.6%	20.6%
Tennessee	132	57.9%	12.4%	−45.5%
Texas	181	38.2%	17.5%	−20.7%
Utah	104	40.0%	21.2%	−18.8%
Vermont	180	100.0%	36.9%	−63.1%
Virginia	140	52.6%	14.0%	−38.6%
Washington	147	35.3%	32.3%	−3.0%
West Virginia	134	66.7%	15.3%	−51.4%
Wisconsin	132	44.4%	20.3%	−24.1%
Wyoming	90	0.0%	17.2%	17.2%

Note: (Negative numbers in the last column indicate where women of color legislators serve at higher proportional rates than white women legislators.)

and Vermont. Of course, this is a function of numbers—there is only one legislator of color in Vermont and only two in Nebraska, all of which are women of color. There are no women of color legislators in Kentucky, Maine, North Dakota, South Dakota, or Wyoming. For white women as a percentage of whites, their proportional representation is lowest in Alabama, where women only constitute 7.5% of white legislators. White women in Hawaii represent 54.5% of all white legislators.

Turning to the differences in proportions, and if we exclude the states where no women of color serve, there are only six states where white women serve at higher proportional rates than do women of color: Alaska, Connecticut, Hawaii, Michigan, Minnesota, and Nevada. Again, this is partially attributed to sheer numbers—smaller numbers of legislators of color overall drive much of this difference in proportion. It could also be a function of the minority population within the state: there are very few minorities in, say, Connecticut. The case of Hawaii, however, makes this conclusion suspect. In the state with the largest minority population, white women legislators are overrepresented as a proportion of white legislators at 54.5%. And, although Hawaii is indeed the state where we saw the highest levels of representation for women of color as noted in Table 1.1, as a proportion of all legislators of color within the state, they constitute only 29.2%.

Overall, if women of color are not doubly disadvantaged, as partially documented by the preceding data, then what processes account for their higher levels of proportional representation? Gender, for women of color, appears to be an advantage, and race/ethnicity is intersecting with gender and elective service. But exactly *where* and *how* they are intersecting is under-explored in terms of legislative office holding. The idea presented in this book contends that the theory of intersectionality helps us in understanding the divergent geographical patterns and gender gaps we witness among different racial/ethnic groups of women. Placing women of color at the center of analysis, I investigate whether our common understanding of the geographical variation and the gender gap in office holding equally explain electoral service by white women and women of color.

The goal is very simple: test *one* set of assumptions within the women and politics literature using an intersectional analysis. The goal may be modest, but the application of this endeavor is not. Collecting intersectional data, even at the state level, is a challenging task, and part of the reason that the aim is humble. It is not intended to answer all of the questions that may arise during the execution of the project. Instead, what I present in this manuscript is basic evidence that gender and race/ethnicity *do* intersect with regard to the gender gap in women's office holding at the state level. As the women and politics literature moves forward, these findings might changes how we theorize about the state-level contexts that influence gender and office holding. In short, I intend this project to provide stepping-stones for further investigation.

OUTLINE OF THE BOOK

Chapter 2 lays out the theoretical arguments, hypotheses, and expectations. I explore the theory of intersectionality more in depth and offer a critical analysis of the current trends in women and politics scholarship on the geographical variation in women's office holding. I also discuss the relevant studies from the race and ethnic politics literature.

From this review of the literature, I develop a hypothetical typology to specify the state-level conditions that might be more or less favorable for legislative service by women of color and offer some explanations for why each indicator may have an impact on white women and women of color differently. For example, some scholars have suggested that women of color have been able to utilize certain institutional level rules and electoral configurations. The Voting Rights Act of 1965 facilitated an exponential increase in the African American voter turnout in the Jim Crow South and a corresponding increase in black representatives via the implementation of majority-minority districts. This particular example is one from which white women would not have benefited.[33] How, and does, this particular feature function in terms of state-level office holding for women of color?

What other state-level factors might contribute to the comparatively heightened levels of office holding by women of color? Carefully following the literature, and based on my own work in this area, I propose that the potential pool of female candidates, the political culture in the state, the level of liberal political ideologies, the percent of the minority population, legislative professionalization, and the presence of multimember districts do not operate in the same way for helping to predict where women of color legislators as compared to white female legislators will serve.[34]

Chapter 3 provides a descriptive picture of the geographical landscape and illustrates the puzzle under investigation by providing a view of where women, white women, women of color, legislators of color, and men of color serve (the latter two of which I include for comparative purposes) and how their proportions have increased and decreased over a particular averaged span of time: 1990 through 2010. I provide a state-by-state snapshot of the data along with a discussion of the top ten and bottom ten states for each of the groups listed earlier.

Looking at the descriptive pattern of representation averaged over the last two decades calls attention to three things. First, women of color legislators tend to cluster in certain states, which is partly explained by the percentage of the minority population within the state.[35] Second, the geographic variation of legislators who are women of color does not perfectly emulate women *or* minority office holding. In other words, where women of color are more or less likely to be present at the state level cannot be determined by looking at the gender or race/ethnicity composition of the state legislatures. Third, exploring the data on the gender gap in office holding by race/ethnicity confirms the first two observations. The white and legislator of color gender gaps in office holding are unevenly disbursed. There are some overlaps, yet the preponderance of the states in either the top ten or bottom ten with regard to the white gender gap states is not the same states when compared to the legislator of color gender gap.

Chapters 4 and 5 then impose statistical tests on observations from Chapter 3. In Chapter 4, utilizing the pooled average of data from five points in time (1990, 1995, 2000, 2005, and 2010), I address whether the same predictors of legislative service operate the same or differently for white women and women of color. In other words, given the geographical variation in women's office holding across the fifty states, what are the chances that a female legislator will be a woman of color? In this way, the findings in Chapter 4 can be interpreted as a racial/ethnic analysis of gender. My evaluation reveals that the conventional wisdom about where women are more or less likely to serve best describes white women's legislative office holding. In terms of explaining the geographical variation of women of color at the state level, only the percentage of the minority population and political culture significantly predict the descriptive representation of women of color. The other factors do not independently influence where we are more or less likely to see women of color legislators. Race/ethnicity is intersecting with gender in terms of state legislative office holding.

Chapter 5 concentrates on another way to slice the data and asks if these same predictors help to explain the smaller racial/ethnic gender gap in office holding. Given the geographical variation in office holding by legislators of color across the fifty states, what are the chances that a legislator of color will be a woman? Hence, the findings in Chapter 5 can be described as a gendered analysis of racial/ethnic. Similar to the conclusions in Chapter 4, the explanatory variables for the white gender gap and the legislator of color gender gap differ quite a bit. The factors that are significantly associated with the white gender gap in state legislative service do not correspond to the gender gap for legislators of color.

The white gender gap decreases in state that have more moralistic political cultures, higher levels of liberal ideologies, less professionalized legislatures, and multimember districts. The legislator of color gender gap, on the other hand, decreases in states with higher percentages of professional women, more Traditionalistic political cultures, multimember districts, *more* professionalized legislatures, and *lower* percentages of minority populations within the state. Here, one of the truly interesting findings within this manuscript is presented: although higher percentages of minority populations in a state *positively* predict whether a female legislator will be a woman of color, they *negatively* predict that a legislator of color will be woman. To say the last part differently, as the percentage of the minority population increases, the legislator of color gender gap also increases. Gender is intersecting with race/ethnicity in terms of state legislative office holding.

Chapter 6 presents some concluding remarks and offers some possible avenues for future research. The evidence presented in this book indicates that perhaps what we know about gender and politics, although not incorrect, is at least conditional. Race/ethnicity and gender are intersecting in the present study, and this intersection influences and challenges our common assumption about where women are more or less likely to serve as state legislators. In short, intersecting models of state legislative office holding may pave the way to a deeper understanding of how gender and race/ethnicity influence descriptive representation. To be sure, this is a complicated and demanding area of research. Nonetheless, as Smooth argues, it is definitely "a mess worth making."[36]

NOTES

1. Kira Sanbonmatsu, *Where Women Run: Gender and Party in the American States* (Ann Arbor: University of Michigan Press, 2006); Laura Elder, "The Partisan Gap Among Women Legislators," *Journal of Women, Politics, and Policy* 33, no. 1 (2012): 65–85; and David Niven, *The Missing Majority: The Recruitment of Women as State Legislative Candidates* (Westport, Connecticut: Praeger, 1998).
2. Center for American Women and Politics, "Women in State Legislatures 2010," New Brunswick, NJ: Eagleton Institute for Politics, Rutgers, State University of New Jersey, 2010, http://www.cawp.rutgers.edu/fast_facts/levels_of_office/documents/stleg.pdf; and Center for American Women and Politics, "Women of Color in Elective Office 2010," New Brunswick, NJ: Eagleton Institute for Politics, Rutgers, State University of New Jersey, 2010, http://www.cawp.rutgers.edu/fast_facts/levels_of_office/documents/color.pdf
3. Zoe M. Oxley and Richard L. Fox, "Women in Executive Office: Variation Across American States," *Political Research Quarterly* 57, no.1 (March 2004): 113–120; Kevin Arceneaux, "The 'Gender Gap' in State Legislative Representation: New Data to Tackle and Old Question," *Political Research Quarterly* 54 (2001): 143–160; Robert E. Hogan, "The Influences of State and District Conditions on the Representation

of Women in U.S. State Legislatures," *American Politics Research* 29 (2001): 4–24; K. Sanbomatsu, *Where Women Run: Gender and Party in the American States*; Jennifer Lawless, *Becoming a Candidate: Political Ambition and the Decision to Run for Office* (New York: Cambridge University Press, 2012); Jennifer Lawless and Richard Fox, *It Still Takes a Candidate: Why Women Don't Run for Office* (New York: Cambridge University Press, 2010); and Jennifer L. Lawless and Richard L. Fox, *It Takes a Candidate: Why Women Don't Run for Office*, (New York: Cambridge University Press, 2005).
4. Marianne Githens and Jewel L. Prestage, *A Portrait of Marginality: The Political Behavior of the American Woman* (New York: David McKay, 1977); Robert Darcy and Charles D. Hadley, "Black Women in Politics: The Puzzle of Success," *Social Science Quarterly* 69, no. 3 (September 1988): 629–645; and Gary Moncrief, Joel Thompson, and Robert Schuhmann, "Gender, Race, and the State Legislature: A Research Note on the Double Disadvantage Hypothesis," *Social Science Journal* 28 (1991): 481–87.
5. For example, see Marsha J. Darling, "African-American Women in State Elective Office in the South," In *Women and Elective Office: Past, Present and Future*, ed. by Sue Thomas and Clyde Wilcox (New York: New York University Press, 1998), 150–162; Diane Prindeville, "Feminist Nations? A Study of Native American Women in Southwestern Tribal Politics," *Political Research Quarterly* 57, no. 1 (2004): 101–112; Diane-Michele Prindeville and Teresa Braley Gomez, "American Indian Women Leaders, Public Policy, and the Importance of Gender and Ethnic Identity," *Women and Politics* 20, no. 2 (1991): 17–32; Kathleen A. Bratton, Kerry L. Haynie, and Beth Reingold, "Agenda Setting and African American Women in State Legislatures" (paper presented at the Annual Meeting of the American Political Science Association, Washington, DC, September 1–4, 2005); Byron Orey and Wendy Smooth, with Kimberly S. Adams and Kisha H. Clark, "Race and Gender Matter: Refining Models of Legislative Policy Making in State Legislatures," *Journal of Women, Politics & Policy* 28, no. 314 (2006): 97–119; Wendy Smooth, "African American Women State Legislators: The Impact of Gender and Race on Legislative Influence," (PhD diss., University of Maryland College Park, 2001); Linda Faye Williams, "The Civil Rights-Black Power Legacy: Black Women Elected Officials at the Local, State, and National Levels," in *Sisters in the Struggle: African American Women in the Civil Rights-Black*

Power Movement, ed. Bettye Collier-Thomas and V. P. Franklin (New York: New York University Press, 2001), 306–331; E. J. Barrett, "The Policy Priorities of African-American Women In State Legislatures," *Legislative Studies Quarterly* 20, no. 2 (May 1995): 223–247; Edith. J. Barrett, "Gender and Race in the State House: The Legislative Experience," *The Social Science Journal* 34, no. 2 (1997): 105–269; Edith J. Barrett, "Black Women in State Legislatures: The Relationship of Race and Gender to the Legislative Experience," in *The Impact of Women in Public Office*, ed. Susan J. Carroll (Bloomington: Indiana University Press, 2001), 185–204; Kathleen A. Bratton and Kerry L. Haynie, "Agenda Setting and Legislative Success in State Legislatures: The Effects of Gender and Race," *The Journal of Politics* 61, no. 3 (1999): 658–679; Bratton, Haynie, and Reingold, "Agenda Setting"; Jewel Prestage, "Black Women State Legislators: A Profile," in *A Portrait of Marginality: The Political Behavior of the American Woman*, ed. M. Githens and J. L. Prestage (New York: David McKay, 1977), 400–418; Luis Ricardo Fraga, Valerie Martinez-Ebers, Linda Lopez, and Ricardo Ramirez, "Strategic Intersectionality: Gender, Ethnicity, and Political Incorporation" (paper delivered at the *Western Political Science Association's* annual meeting, Oakland, CA, March 17–19, 2005); and Luis Ricardo Fraga, Linda Lopez, Valerie Martinez-Ebers, and Ricardo Ramirez, "Gender and Ethnicity: Patterns of Electoral Success and Legislative Advocacy Among Latina and Latino State Officials in Four States," *Journal of Women, Politics and Policy* 28, no. 3–4 (2006):122–145.

6. Katie E. Ostrander and Pei-te Lien, "Structural and Contextual Factors in the Election of Women and Minorities to Sub-National Offices: A Review of the Literature" (paper presented at the Annual Meeting of the Western Political Science Association, San Francisco, April 1–3, 2010); Cathy J. Cohen, "A Portrait of Marginality: The Study of Women of Color in American Politics," in *Women and American Politics: New Questions, New Directions*, ed. Susan J. Carroll (Oxford: Oxford University Press, 2003); Edith J. Barrett, "Black Women"; and Lisa J. Montoya, Carol Hardy-Fanta, and Sonia Garcia, "Latina Politics: Gender, Participation, and Leadership," *PS: Political Science and Politics* 33, no. 3 (September 2000): 555–561.

7. Rogers Smith, *Civic Ideals: Conflicting Visions of Citizenship in U.S. History* (New Haven, CT: Yale University Press, 1997); Ian Haney López, *White by Law: The Legal Construction of Race* (New York: New York University Press, 2006);

and Carol Pateman, *The Disorder of Women: Democracy, Feminism, and Political Theory* (Palo Alto, CA: Stanford University Press, 1989).
8. Hanna Fenichel Pitkin, *The Concept of Representation* (Berkeley: University of California Press, 1967), 144.
9. Ibid., 61 (italics in original).
10. Ibid., 144.
11. Ibid., 212.
12. However, Mansbridge notes that our representative institutions serve two functions: deliberative, which involves questions of process, and aggregative, which involves questions of outcome. For the deliberative aspect, Mansbridge says that one's voice must be reflected in the debate. Mansbridge argues that we are more likely to get aggregate democratic outcomes when the deliberative process is descriptively representative of the population.

    See Jane Mansbridge, "Should Women Represent Women and Blacks Represent Blacks? A Contingent 'Yes,'" *Journal of Politics* 61, no. 3 (August 1999), 628–657. See also Suzanne Dovi, "Preferable Descriptive Representatives: Will Just Any Woman, Black, or Latino Do?" *American Political Science Review* 96, no. 4 (December 2002): 729–743; and Virginia Sapiro, "When Are Interests Interesting? The Problem of Political Representation of Women," *American Political Science Review* 75 (September 1981): 701–16 (reprinted in *Feminism and Politics*, ed. Anne Phillips [New York: Oxford University Press, 1998]), 161–192 for a discussion of when, why, and how gender should matter in terms of substantive representation and how female representatives might fulfill this aspect and function of representative in our legislative bodies.
13. Verba, Burns, and Schlozman noted difference between women and men in terms of working on a campaign (8% to 9%), contributing to a campaign (21% to 29%), contacting a government official (30% to 38%), and affiliating with a political organization (44% to 53%). Although women have registered and voted at higher rates than men since 1980, these are the only two acts of political participation where women participate politically more than men. See Sidney Verba, Nancy Burns, and Kay Lehman Schlozman, "Knowing and Caring about Politics: Gender and Political Engagement," *Journal of Politics* 59, no. 4 (November 1997): 1051–1072. However, Baxter and Lansing and Williams note that black women have voted at higher rates than black men in presidential elections since 1976 and 1974, respectively.

See Sandra Baxter and Marjorie Lansing, *Women and Politics: The Visible Majority* (Ann Arbor: University of Michigan Press, 1983); and Williams, "The Civil Rights-Black Power Legacy."

14. But see Carole Uhlaner, Katie Cooper, and Becki Scola, "Descriptive Representation and Voter Turnout in the U.S.: Effects of the Intersection of Gender, Race and Ethnicity," Unpublished Manuscript, (2013) for a discussion of how this varies by race, gender, and the intersection of both in terms of voting and registration across the fifty states.

15. Craig Leonard Brians, "Women for Women? Gender and Party Bias in Voting for Female Candidates," *American Politics Research* 33, no. 3 (May 2005): 357–375; and Brian F. Schaffner, "Priming Gender: Campaigning on Women's Issues in U.S. Senate Elections," *American Journal of Political Science* 49, no. 4 (October 2005): 803–817.

16. Claudine Gay, "The Effect of Black Congressional Representation on Political Participation," *American Political Science Review* 95 no. 3 (2001): 589–602; Matt A. Barreto, "¡Sí Se Puede! Latino Candidates and the Mobilization of Latino Voters," *American Political Science Review* 101, no. 3 (August 2007): 425–441; Lawrence Bobo and Franklin D. Gilliam, "Race, Sociopolitical Participation, and Black Empowerment," *American Political Science Review* 84 (1990): 377–393; Rufus P. Browning, Dale Rogers Marshall, David H. Tabb, *Racial Politics in American Cities*, 3rd ed. (Upper Saddle River, NJ: Pearson, 2002); and Christopher Stout and Katherine Tate, "The 2008 Presidential Election, Political Efficacy, and Group Empowerment," *Politics, Groups, and Identities* 1, no. 2 (2013): 143–163.

17. Marsha Matson and Terri Susan Fine, "Gender, Ethnicity, and Ballot Information: Ballot Cues in Low-Information Elections," *State Politics and Policy Quarterly* 6, no. 1 (Spring 2006): 49–72; and Stout and Tate, "The 2008 Presidential Election," 157 (italics added).

18. See, for instance, Sue Thomas, "The Impact of Women on State Legislative Policies," *Journal of Politics* 53, no. 4 (1991): 958–976; Sue Thomas, "Women in State Legislatures: One Step at a Time," in *The Year of the Woman: Myths and Realities*, ed. Elizabeth Adell Cook, Sue Thomas, and Clyde Wilcox (San Francisco: Westview Press, 1994), 148–155; Debra L. Dodson, ed., *Gender and Policymaking: Studies of Women in Office* (New Brunswick, NJ: Center for American Women and Politics, Eagleton Institute of Politics, Rutgers, the State University of New Jersey, 1991); Susan J. Carroll,

"Representing Women: Women State Legislators as Agents of Policy-Related Change," in *The Impact of Women in Public Office*, ed. Susan J. Carroll (Bloomington: Indiana University Press, 2001), 3–21; Michele L. Swers, *The Difference Women Make: The Policy Impact of Women on Congress* (Chicago: University of Chicago Press, 2002); and Sue Thomas and Susan Welch, "The Impact of Women in State Legislatures: Numerical and Organizational Strength," in *The Impact of Women in Public Office*, ed. Susan J. Carroll (Bloomington: Indiana University Press, 2001), 166–181.

19. See, for example, Kerry Haynie, *African American State Legislators in the American States* (New York: Columbia University Press, 2001); Katherine Tate, *Black Faces in the Mirror: African Americans and Their Representatives in the U.S. Congress* (Chicago: University of Chicago Press, 2003); and David T. Canon, *Race, Redistricting, and Representation: The Unintended Consequences of Black Majority Districts* (Chicago: University of Chicago Press, 1999).
20. Lynne E. Ford and Kathleen Dolan, "Women State Legislators: Three Decades of Gains in Representation and Diversity," in *Women and Politics: Outsiders or Insiders? A Collection of Readings*, ed. Lois Lovelace Duke (Upper Saddle River, NJ: Prentice Hall, 1999), 203–218.
21. Ibid., 205.
22. For example, laws regarding marriage, education, and reproduction health are primarily decided at the state level, the last of which has again become a highly contested issue, especially at the state level. Trounstine argues that "[i]n the United States a large proportion of political activity occurs at the sub-state level. The vast majority of elected officials are local legislators" and that "[l]ocal decisions and policies also account for a large and growing proportion of total government activity" See Jessica Trounstine, "All Politics is Local: The Reemergence of the Study of City Politics," *Perspectives on Politics* 7, no. 3 (September 2009): 612.
23. Ostrander and Lien, "Structural and Contextual Factors"; Malcom E. Jewell, *Representation in State Legislatures* (Lexington: University of Kentucky Press, 1982); and Christopher Z. Mooney, "State Politics and Policy Quarterly and the Study of State Politics: The Editor's Introduction," *State Politics and Policy Quarterly* (Spring 2001): 1–4.
24. Ostrander and Lien, "Structural and Contextual Factors," 4.
25. Center for American Women and Politics, "Women in State Legislatures 2010"; and Center for American Women and Politics, "Women of Color in Elective Office 2010."

26. For the purposes of this book, legislators of color, women of color, and men of color are defined as the combination of the racial and ethnic U.S. Census Bureau categories of African Americans, Latinos, Asian Pacific Americans, and Native Americans. The author understands the problematic nature of this classification. The terms are operationalized in this manner to increase the total number of women of color legislators in each state for statistical analysis. It is not meant to imply that all racial and ethnic groups or women of color are the same. More explanation for collapsing the data in this manner can be found in Chapter 3, where I provide a more detailed account of the dependent variables utilized in this manuscript.
27. See Wilma Rule and Pippa Norris, "Anglo and Minority Women's Underrepresentation in Congress: Is the Electoral System the Culprit?" In *United States Electoral Systems: Their Impact on Women and Minorities*, ed. Wilma Rule and Joseph F. Zimmerman (New York: Greenwood Press, 1992), 41–54; and Susan Welch and Rebekah Herrick, "The Impact of At-Large Elections on the Representation of Minority Women," in *United States Electoral Systems: Their Impact on Women and Minorities*, ed. Wilma Rule and Joseph F. Zimmerman (New York: Greenwood Press, 1992), 153–166.
28. Sources for all of the data presented in this chapter include Center for American Women and Politics, National Council for State Legislatures, the Joint Center, the National Association for Latino Elected Officials, and UCLA's Asian American Studies Center.
29. If we take Hawaii out, the next highest percentage of legislators of color can be found in New Mexico, at 50.9%, followed by California at 32.5% and Texas at 30.4%. For men of color, New Mexico is also the next highest for their legislative service, at 34.8%, followed by Mississippi at 21.3%. See Chapter 3 for a state-by-state discussion of these numbers.
30. Githens and Prestage, *A Portrait of Marginality*; Darcy and Hadley, "Black Women in Politics"; and Moncrief, Thompson, and Schuhmann, "Gender, Race, and the State Legislature."
31. Moncrief, Thompson, and Schuhmann, "Gender, Race, and the State Legislature," 485.
32. Darcy and Hadley, "Black Women in Politics"; Harry Pachon and Louis DeSipio, "Latino Elected Officials in the 1990s," *PS: Political Science and Politics* 25, no. 2 (June 1991): 212–217; R. Darcy, Susan Welch, and Janet Clark. 1994. *Women, Elections, and Representation*, 2nd ed. (Lincoln: Nebraska

University Press, 1994); Paule Cruz Takash, "Breaking Barriers to Representation: Chicana/Latina Elected Officials in California," in *Women Transforming Politics: An Alternative Reader*, ed. Cathy J. Cohen, Kathleen B. Jones, and Joan C. Tronto (New York: New York University Press, 1997), 412–434; Montoya, Hardy-Fanta, and Garcia, "Latina Politics"; Fraga et al., "Gender and Ethnicity: Patterns of Electoral Success"; and Tate, *Black Faces in the Mirror*.
33. Darcy and Hadley, "Black Women in Politics"; Smooth, "African American Women State Legislators"; and Tate, *Black Faces in the Mirror*.
34. Becki Scola, "Predicting Presence at the Intersections: Assessing the Variation in Women's Office Holding across the States," *State Politics & Policy Quarterly* 13(3) (2013): 333–348; Becki Scola, "Women of Color in State Legislatures: Gender, Race, and Legislative Office Holding," *Journal of Women, Politics, and Policy* 28, no. 3–4 (2006): 43–70.
35. Chapter 4 discusses this finding in more detail. In short, however, although the percentage of the minority population is a significant predictor of where women of color serve, political culture is also useful for explaining their geographical variation.
36. Wendy Smooth, "Intersectionality in Electoral Politics: A Mess Worth Making," *Politics & Gender* 2, no. 3 (2006): 400–414.

2 Geographical Variation, the Gender Gap, and Intersecting Theories of Representation

As discussed in Chapter 1, it was reasonable to assume an upward trend in women's office holding as time passed. In other words, as women entered the workforce, colleges, and the professions at higher rates, there would be a continual increase in women's office holding. But, women are entering and graduating college at record numbers—numbers that outpace men's educational attainment. More women are pursuing professional careers than ever before. The pool of potential women office holders is there, yet, we see quite a few states where women's office holding has reached a plateau, and in a few state legislatures, women's legislative service has actually declined. At this point in time, we might say that these individual-level indicators have encountered a diminishing margin of return—more qualified women in the pool of potential candidates, but these improvements are not yielding the expected (or desired) effect of increasing women's office holding. Clearly, something else is going on.

Previous studies have suggested a range of potential factors that may contribute to the gender gap in office holding. Although there has been popular debate on the viability of female candidates and an ever-expanding literature on women's campaign strategies and tactics, several studies have documented that women win just as often, if not more so, than similarly situated male candidates. In other words, "when women run, they win."[1] In fact, the discrepancy we see in the numerical representation of women is not due to the public evaluating a female candidate unfavorably, a woman candidate's inability to raise money, or the electorate's unwillingness to vote for a female representative.[2]

Since the electoral environment appears to be fairly favorable for women candidates (when they run, they win), we might reasonably conclude that this is not the process that accounts for the disparity we see in office holding. What does, then?

Some scholars have said that the problem is that *women do not run*.[3] In a nutshell, women have less ambition than men to run for public office. Others studies have indicated that there are state-level contexts and legislative characteristics that have an impact on the election of women. If these are both true, then what explains the differences we see among the percentages of white women legislators and women of color legislators? Are women of color more ambitious? Do the institutional features affect white women and women of color differently? Why? The question of ambition is an entirely separate question and is discussed briefly in the concluding remarks in Chapter 6. Here, my goal is to investigate the terrain of the gender gap across the states and develop some hypotheses about how this knowledge applies to women of color legislators.

The next section takes a closer, but brief, look at the work on the geographical variation of female legislators—the "conventional wisdom" in terms of where we are more or less likely to see women office holders and what assists us in understanding the gender gap at the state level. At this point it is important to note that looking at the cross-sectional variation in state legislative office holding is, *in and of itself*, a measurement of the gender gap among state legislators because the dependent variable is the percentage of women within state legislatures—the conventional wisdom explains both the geographical variation and the gender gap simultaneously. I use two terms interchangeable when discussing the variation of women's office holding across the states—*geographical* and/or *cross-section variation*. However, when discussing the gender gap disaggregated by race/ethnicity, I am no longer measuring the variation, per se, of women, white or of color, across the states. Instead, I measure the variation in the parity between men and women within their respective racial/ethnic group. Hence, I use the terms *white gender gap* and *legislator of color gender gap* to differentiate between the tests for geographical variation among different groups of women.

My goal in the end is to investigate how this conventional wisdom applies to the presence of women of color state legislators and the smaller racial/ethnic gender gap in office holding. Do the factors that influence the variation we see in female legislative service across the states vary by race/ethnicity? Do these factors also help us in explaining the smaller gender gap among legislators of color? From the perspective of the theory of intersecting identities, I argue that, if we disaggregate women legislators by race/ethnicity, not all factors will accurately predict the presence of white female legislators and women of color legislators as effectively as they do when we do not account for the race/ethnicity of female office holders.

EXPLAINING WOMEN'S UNDERREPRESENTATION AT THE STATE LEVEL

Scholars in the field of women and politics have taken different paths to studying the descriptive representation of women at the state level. Some have accounted for the change over time in state legislatures, others have looked at particular features of a state such as political parties, and some have directly investigated the cross-sectional variation in women's office holding.[4] For comparability purposes, the findings from these latter studies are what guide the current project, and I focus specifically on the factors that have consistently explained the variation across states within these equivalent investigations.[5] First, I review these articles of interest before offering a summary of the most commonly significant variables among the analyses. These indicators serve as the independent variables for the current project.

Palmer and Simon state that "[t]here are surprisingly few analyses of geography and demography and their impact on women's success. As a result, we know very little about the districts *where* women win."[6] Although Palmer and Simon are specifically talking about congressional districts, the same can be said for state houses. Generally speaking, however, earlier work on women's geographical variation in state legislatures leads us to expect higher levels of female office holding in states with a certain mix of demographic, contextual, and institutional structures. For example, starting with Hill's study of how political culture has an impact on the variation of women in state legislatures, his regression results of forty-eight states in 1973 demonstrates that, although the institutional factors of compensation and constituency size are significant, "[Moralistic] political culture is substantially more influential than structures in determining female presence in the state legislatures."[7] Nechemias's longitudinal study focused on "three time periods—1963–1964, 1971–1972, and 1983–1984."[8] Using institutional indicators similar to Hill, Nechemias also includes party dominance, per capita income, and urbanization as well as a control for southern states. Her bivariate analysis suggests that the contextual and cultural characteristics of level of education within the population and moralistic political culture are most correlated with the election of women.

Rule explores a variety of factors in an investigation of the variation in women in legislatures across the fifty states from 1974 to 1984.[9] She finds that the most powerful positive predictors of women's election to state legislative office are a combination of characteristics: the historical presence of women in office, the percentage of women statewide officials, percentage of professional women in the electorate, single-primary states, multimember districts, and the presence of National Organization for Women (NOW) organizations within the state. Among the negative institutional predictors are Democratic dominance and states with Traditionalistic cultures. Similarly, Norrander and Wilcox studied factors that affected women's presence in state legislative office for 1995.[10] They determine that certain indicators in all three categories of variables are significant: "the best predictors of women's presence in state legislatures are ideology of the state, political culture, the proportion of women in the candidate pool, multimember districts, level of turnover, and . . . the proportions of conservative Protestant religious denominations."[11]

More recently, Hogan conducts a logistical regression analysis of legislative seats in 1995 using several district- and state-level indicators.[12] He finds that the following indicators are positively related to the probability that a woman is elected to a state legislative seat: states with Moralistic and Individualistic cultures, a higher percentage of women in the chamber, multimember districts, a higher educational levels in the district, a higher percentage of white-collar workers in the district, and a higher percentages of a district's minority population. Indicators negatively associated with the election of women to state legislative seats include legislatures that are more professional and districts that are larger. Arceneaux's model finds that Moralistic culture, liberal political ideology, feminist attitudes, multimember districts, and high proportions of women in the labor force have a positive impact on the percentage of women in the state legislature.[13] The attractiveness of the office measured as legislative salary, on the other hand, has a negative impact on women's presence.

Across these studies, I identified five variables that were consistently used and were found to be significant for predicting the geographical variation in women's office holding, which I discuss more fully in the subsections that follow. Then, I discuss why applying an intersectional framework to the gender gap in office holding may present different results.

Potential Pool of Female Candidates

The presence of a sufficient recruitment pool of women is essential—there needs to be an adequate cluster of qualified, potential candidates from which women leaders can emerge. Women with higher levels of education, income, and workforce experience not only have a larger set of resources from which to draw if they decide to run for political office, but they are also more likely to be encouraged and recruited to seek political office.[14] Indeed, studies suggest that these factors positively relate to the cross-sectional variation in female state legislators.[15] States where women have higher levels of education and higher levels of workforce participation are positively related to the percentage of female legislators at the state level.[16]

Political Culture

Politics and people's approach to politics differs depending on the region and political culture of a state. Elazar defines political culture as "the particular pattern of orientation to political action in which each political system is imbedded."[17] Within the literature, states with Moralistic political cultures are cited as being more likely to elect women to public office due to the electorate's innovative and progressive approach to politics, which is contrasted to a Traditionalistic state's emphasis on preserving the status quo.[18] In fact, this particular variable is the most consistent across studies in helping us understand the geographical variation in women's office holding. It is always a significant predictor in the direction of states classified as having a Moralistic political culture.

Liberal Ideology and Minority Populations

Some women and politics scholars have suggested that states with higher levels of liberal ideologies and higher percentages of minority populations are more likely to have higher percentages of women in their legislatures.[19] The argument here is fairly straightforward—states where a larger majority of the population leans more toward the left are more intent on and supportive of including members of disadvantaged groups into the public realm. Similarly, it is theorized that traditionally marginalized populations are more open to non-traditional groups' increased participation in social, economic, and political arenas, as they are more likely to feel an affinity with a person from a similarly situated group.[20] Both of these state-level indicators are positively related to higher levels of women legislators.[21]

Professionalized Legislatures

Highly professionalized legislatures (those with high salaries, large staffs, and longer sessions) might make a legislative career more attractive, which in turn may generate an increase in male candidates, putting potential female hopefuls at a disadvantage.[22] Then again, men, on average, have higher incomes than do women in the private sector, which suggests that men encounter a higher opportunity cost when they run for office. Nevertheless, the literature supports the idea that we will see fewer women in more professional legislatures, although this finding seems to depend on the context and time frame under investigation.[23]

To summarize, the model derived from earlier work on the cross-sectional variation of women in state legislatures provides us with five consistently used, comparable factors that best predict the presence of female office holders: pool of candidates, political culture, political ideology, minority population, and legislative professionalization. Do these predictors differ if we take the race/ethnicity of the female legislator into account? In other words, does the model explain the variation we see in office holding by both white women and women of color?

In the following section, I suggest that the theory of intersecting identities provides us with a good reason to suspect that the model may not be as useful in helping us understand the range in the sex composition of state legislatures if we disaggregate by race/ethnicity. I then move on to a fuller discussion of women of color legislators specifically before presenting an intersectional approach for assessing geographical variation and the smaller gender gap in office holding by women of color.

INTERSECTING IDENTITIES IN THEORY AND PRACTICE

Intersectionality theorists contend that women have multiple identities that inform political activity. They are not just "women" or "minorities"—they are both simultaneously.[24] Mansbridge and Tate contend that "[r]ace and gender are intimately intertwined in the lives of Black women in the United States. Race constructs the way Black women experience gender; gender constructs the way Black women experience race."[25] Therefore, scholars cannot fully describe, study, and understand political phenomenon without addressing the multiple identities that give rise to these experiences.

To be sure, several women and politics scholars have employed an intersectional framework to study how race and gender intersect at the elite level in terms of background characteristics and political ambition, as well as at the mass-public level in terms of public opinion and candidate support.[26] Other studies have documented how race intersects with gender at the judicial level.[27]

Smooth applies the theory to the context of the Voting Rights Act and highlights how our traditional understanding of electoral politics changes when viewed through an intersectional lens.[28] Hawkesworth contends that Congress itself is a "raced-gendered institution" that produces "raced and gendered hierarchies that structure interactions among member as well as institutional practices."[29] She suggests further exploring the within-group differences among women to more fully explain the processes that create and maintain both gender and racial hierarchies.

Hence, the theory of intersectionality might lead us to expect that the factors cited as most important in predicting female presence within state legislatures will vary based on the within-group difference of race/ethnicity as well. From this theoretical perspective, I hypothesize that the indicators most commonly used in explaining the variation in women's office holding across the states will not perform equally in predicting the range of legislative service by both white women and women of color. Disaggregating female legislators by race/ethnicity highlights how race intersects with gender as a politically relevant characteristic. Indeed, there is evidence that these intersecting identities matter at the congressional level.[30]

Palmer and Simon determine that the congressional districts that elect white women and black women are distinct regarding sociodemographic and institutional characteristics.[31] In another study, Palmer and Simon add Latinos to their sample and document "many differences . . . in the districts that have elected African American men compared to women . . . even among majority-minority districts" and that "there are clear differences between the districts electing Hispanic Democratic men compared to women."[32] Although Palmer and Simon also note that these differences "are not as numerous as the distinctions between those electing white/non-Hispanic men compared to women," their findings are illustrative for the current project.[33] Palmer and Simon's intersectional analysis highlights that "women-friendly" congressional districts are distinct if the race/ethnicity of the legislator is taken into account. Although race trumps gender to a certain degree, in that there is less difference between districts that elected men and women of color compared to all men and women, there *are* still variations in the types of districts electing male and female legislators of color. Gender matters as well.

An excellent example of how the intersectional approach adds nuance to our analyses at the state level is the case of term limits. Theoretically, terms limits should positively influence the election of women and minorities since the incumbency advantage significantly contributes to the underrepresentation both women and minorities. Incumbents are primarily white males, so the removal of this barrier should support the election of underrepresented groups. Research on whether term limits assist or hinder women is at odds, however, with most studies concluding that term limits may help women only after they are first implemented—the effect seems to diminish the longer that they have been in place.[34]

Of interest here is the intersectional effect of term limits. Carroll and Jenkins note that in 1998, women lost, minorities gained, and women of color "more closely resemble the patterns for women than ... minorities."[35] Furthermore, they carefully note that this pattern varies by race/ethnicity and by year: black women lost seats, and Latinas gained seats. In contrast, for the 2000 election, "the pattern for minority women parallels the pattern for minorities more generally" for both black women and Latinas.[36] The study of how term limits have an impact on female office holding are frequently included in studies that look at the increase in female representation over time and not typically present in projects that look directly at the variation. In other words, because the current investigation is grounded in the variation literature and does not attempt to explain change over time in women's office holding, term limits are not included in the analysis. Nevertheless, this intersecting illustration of term limits provides leverage for the idea that the five variables under investigation in this study might vary as well.

WOMEN OF COLOR AT THE CENTER

Scholars contend that women of color as political elites are often overlooked and neglected, and as a result, we have very little research on women of color elected officials.[37] Cammisa and Reingold claim that "the research on women state legislators effectively has been about white women only" and that "women of color remain largely invisible in the scholarly literature on women in state legislatures."[38] Ostrander and Lien advise that "[g]iven the relative dearth of women of color holding elective offices and as research subjects, it is safe to assume, unless otherwise specified, that the term 'women' primarily refers to white women, the term 'minorities' to males who are blacks and, to a small extent, Latinos."[39] What we do know about the politics of women of color is primarily descriptive or at the level of participation, with studies concluding that women of color engage in politics for different reasons than both white women and men of color.[40]

Studies looking specifically at women of color state legislators tend to focus on how they perform their role as a legislator and the reasons for their entrance into more formal channels of electoral politics as compared to their white female and male of color counterparts, the latter of which is discussed briefly in Chapter 6.[41] According to these studies, women of color legislators exhibit legislative behavior and attitudes at the intersection of race and gender, with both identities influencing their policy goals, their agendas, and their interaction with constituents.

Smooth notes that women of color have outpaced both white women and men of color over the last decade in terms of legislative office holding.[42] This begs the question of why the intersection of gender and race have been politically relevant for women of color over the last ten years, but the separate categories of gender (white women) and race (men of color) have lost their political punch. And, while it has been well documented that women of color serve in our electoral institutions in relatively higher proportions than white women, only a handful of studies have attempted to answer why women of color experience higher rates of representation.[43] Furthermore, most factors fail to fully explain the variation across the states or the differences between groups of women.

In regards to differential proportion between white women and black women, Darcy and Hadley study black and white female Democratic delegates and suggest that "the [greater] electoral success of black women appears to be their greater political ambition derived from their having more politically relevant backgrounds . . . [and] the political opportunities resulting from the Voting Rights Act of 1965," both of which discount the double-disadvantage hypothesis.[44] Moncrief, Thompson, and Schuhmann also find in an investigation of the descriptive patterns in eleven state legislatures that black women legislators have higher levels of education and have worked in "higher prestige" occupations in comparison to white women legislators.[45] It seems that potential pool of candidates (education, profession) as well as institutional/context variables (Voter Rights Act provisions) are important for black women's office holding in comparison to their white female counterparts.

Fraga et al. in an investigation of four states (Arizona, California, New Mexico, and Texas) assess "if the electoral gains of women and members of ethnic groups also result in similar success for women of color."[46] Important is that the authors specifically "consider the role of differences in institutional contexts such as majority-party status, size of the legislature, term limits, and legislative professionalization."[47] Although they find mixed results among the four states from 1990 to 2004, they maintain that "although notable growth in both overall gender and Latino representation occurs, the greatest growth by far occurs in Latina representation . . . far outpacing the increases in either gender or overall Latino representation . . . despite significant differences in state political context."[48]

In short, studies that investigate some version of the double-disadvantage hypothesis come up short.[49] Gender for black women and Latinas appears to be an advantage. What is also clear is that the pattern of legislative service by women of color does not mirror their white female counterparts or their racial/ethnic counterparts. Darcy and Hadley along with Moncrief, Thompson, and Schuhmann suggest that black women adhere to a pattern distinct from white women, and Fraga et al. advise that Latinas find themselves in a unique position as well.[50]

What is interesting is that few studies fully investigate the smaller gender gap in office holding for legislators of color across all fifty states—of the studies that actually investigate women of color legislators, very few provide analysis beyond descriptive correlations or case studies in particular states. And, as I discuss in the following, only one study within the race and ethnic politics literature attempts to systematically predict minority electoral service, specifically Latinos, while also accounting for other factors that may influence office holding.

LEGISLATORS OF COLOR AND REPRESENTATION IN THE STATES

Within the women and politics literature reviewed earlier, none of the studies on the state-level geographical variation of female legislators looks at the race/ethnicity of the female office holder. Does the literature race and ethnic politics offer any clues as to where we might see more legislators of color and, hence, more women of color? Yes, but only to a certain extent. Most work on legislators of color is concerned with their experience as office holders and the substantive representation of minority interests regarding policy responsiveness, roll-call voting, and agenda setting.[51] Furthermore, an overwhelming majority of these studies focuses on Congress, and typically, there is not a robust discussion of how gender has an impact on the findings. Minta notes that "the literatures in women and minority political representation have mostly developed in relative isolation from each other, with each focusing exclusively on race or gender but usually not both."[52] But even at the state level, and where the intersection of race and gender is the focus, there is the same pattern of concentration on the substantive representation of minority interests.[53]

Looking specifically at the geographical variation in state legislators of color, there are a few studies from which to draw conclusions. Perhaps the most important factor for explaining the increase in minority representation since 1990 is the creation of majority-minority districts provisioned by the Voting Rights Act (VRA). An overwhelming majority of legislators of color represent majority-minority districts.[54] In fact, in their study on the impact of the VRA on minority office holding for 2006, Lien et al. found "that the vast majority of [nonwhite] state legislators were elected from districts covered by the VRA."[55] This is echoed throughout the literature on legislators of color. At all levels of office holding, the percentage of the minority population within the electorate is highly associated with minority representation.[56]

Cavanagh and Stockton suggest, however, that there are other factors at play such as the strength of party organizations, electoral structures, and the socioeconomic status of the black electorate.[57] In their Joint Center report, Cavanagh and Stockton noted that stronger party structures, at-large elections, and lower levels of black socioeconomic status all have a negative impact on the likelihood that a black representative is elected.

Casellas offers the most comparable analysis for my purposes.[58] Looking at the factors that have an impact on the descriptive representation of Latinos in state legislatures, he finds that states with higher levels of liberal ideology and higher percentages of Latino populations significantly predict Latino representation. Regarding professionalized legislatures, he discovered that the level of professionalization in a state legislature is not significant on its own. But when interacted with the percentage of Latino citizens, Casellas notes that "[s]tates with higher proportions of Latino citizens and less professional legislatures are significantly associated with higher proportion of Latinos in legislatures."[59]

Overall, the findings compare relatively well to the women and politics literature: institutional contexts as well as state/district characteristics have a significant effect on minority representation. First, similar to the women and politics literature that predicts female representation, race and ethnic politics scholars consistently note that the percentage of the minority population is the most significant predictor of minority representation. The higher the minority population, the more likely a state or a district will be represented by a legislator of color. The interesting question here is if and how these variables differentially influence the presence of both women and men of color. I am not arguing with the obvious fact that states with higher minority populations elect more minorities. What is relevant to this particular study is how these findings relate to the variation of women of color legislators and whether this is a significant predictor of the racial/ethnic gender gap in office holding. For example, Barrett found that "the racial composition of the districts of black women are similar to those of black men."[60] Does this finding bear fruit when regressed with other possible factors?

Second, and similar to studies on state-level gender gap, both liberal ideology and legislative professionalization seem to affect minority representation. At least in the case of Latinos, and controlling for other factors, higher levels of liberal ideology and lower levels of legislative professionalization predict higher percentages of Latino legislators.

To be clear, my goal in this project is to test the conventional wisdom within the women and politics literature about the *geographical variation in women's office holding across the states*. For comparability purposes, I have been careful to include only the variables that have been consistently used within those studies and found to be significant. My intent is to use this model from an intersectional perspective as a way to understand legislative service by women of color, the primary question of which is why they are serving at proportionally higher rates than their white female counterparts are.

Hence, what is gleaned from the race and ethnic politics literature *that specifically relates to the geographical variation within state legislatures* does not significantly alter the model derived from the women and politics literature on the geographical variation in women's legislative service. The set of variables that are the most consistently employed *and* found to be significant within that literature offers only one additional item of interest that should be included in my hypotheses about the factors that will best predict legislative service by women of color—the impact of the VRA. Again, scholars consistently cite this particular institutional feature, and the electoral structures that it has produced, as one of the most important for explaining the increase in minority office holding. It is also credited as a possible reason for why women of color have proportionally higher levels of office holding compared to white women.[61]

PREDICTING PRESENCE AT THE INTERSECTION

To summarize, although women and politics scholars have analyzed the cross-sectional variation in the percentage of female legislators, they have not looked at how race/ethnicity influences these findings from a within-group perspective. Within the women and politics literature, most studies agree that women are more likely to serve in states that have larger pools of potential candidates, Moralistic cultures, liberal political ideologies, higher percentages of minority populations, and less professionalized legislatures. These five variables have been the most consistently significant in explaining the geographical variation in women's office holding across the states.

Similarly, very few studies within the race and ethnic politics literature that examines predictors of minority office holding assess how gender has an impact on the results of their studies. Here, scholars of race and ethnic politics offer four variables that are most important for understanding where minorities serve at the state legislative level: higher percentages of minority populations, liberal ideologies, less professionalized legislatures, VRA provisions.

The theory of intersectionality has been applied to many other instances of women's political experience, but it has not been applied in a systematic way to women's variation in office holding across the states. What is documented by the handful of studies that look at predictors of state legislative service suggest that women of color do not perfectly mirror their white female or race/ethnic male counterparts. If only race/ethnicity were at play, then the factors that help us to understand the increase in minority office holding since the 1980s would explain legislative service by both men and women of color. In other words, we would see equal number of men and women of color legislators. As documented by

Darcy and Hadley, Fraga et al., Smooth, and others, women of color are increasing their representational numbers, but men of color are not.[62]

If only gender were at play, then the indicators that explain women's office holding across the state would equally predict where we see both higher levels of white women and women of color. In other words, we would see an equal number of both white women and women of color legislators in proportion to their male racial/ethnic counterparts—there would *be* no racial/ethnic gender gap. But, the data suggest otherwise. And, women and politics scholars have lamented the stagnation in women's legislative numbers over the last twenty years.

So, given what we know, how does this apply to women of color? Can states be categorized as more "favorable" or "not so favorable" for women of color legislators? Utilizing an intersectional framework for assessing the variation would allow us a better understanding of how both gender and race/ethnicity inform the representational outline of our state legislative institutions. This configuration also permits an examination of the smaller racial/gender gap in office holding. If these factors map on to the geographical variation in terms of how they differ for white females and women of color, then they should also be a good starting place for thinking about how these processes differ by race/ethnicity.

Expectations and Typology of Intersectional Representation at the State Level

Through an intersectional perspective, my aim is to test the conventional wisdom within the women and politics literature on the geographical variation in women's state-legislative office. As such, in the following, I list a set of hypotheses that directly follow from the literature. Each hypothesis has three parts. Part "a" reestablishes what the conventional wisdom suggest about women's office holding without differentiating for race/ethnicity. Parts "b" and "c" then predict how I expect each factor to vary, or not, for white female and for women of color legislators.

The potential pool of candidates consistently predicts female office holding across the states. Typically, this is measured by looking at one or more of the following indicators: the percentage of women with higher education, percentage of women in the workforce, and/or the percentage of women in professional occupations. Of course, all three of these are highly correlated. To overcome any potential correlational problems associated with these three indicators, my measure for this variable will be the percentage of professional women in the state. Arguably, a woman who has a professional career has a higher education and is in the workforce, thereby capturing the effect of all three of these indicators in one variable.

I hypothesize that the current study will confirm the positive and significant effect of this variable for predicting female legislative service, but that the results will be greater for women of color legislators than white women. The primary reason to anticipate a stronger influence for women of color is based on findings from previous research, which notes that women of color legislators have higher levels of education than do their white female counterparts.[63] This suggests that the pool of candidates from which women of color emerge is perhaps more affluent when compared directly to the pools of white women at the state level.

H1a: States with higher levels of professional women will have higher percentages of female legislators.
H1b: States with higher levels of professional women will have higher percentages of white female legislators.
H1c: States with higher levels of professional women will have higher percentages of women of color legislators.

For political culture, women of color legislators are concentrated mainly in the southern and western regions of the United States—states that are generally designated as Traditionalistic and Individualistic. White women's office holding is more prominent in the northeastern and midwestern United States—states that are typically designated as Moralistic. Hence, my expectation is that states that are identified as having a Moralistic political culture will positively and significantly relate to white women's legislative service, but will negatively predict service in state legislatures by women of color.

> H2a: States with Moralistic political cultures will have higher percentages of female legislators.
>
> H2b: States with Moralistic political cultures will have higher percentages of white female legislators.
>
> H2c: States with Moralistic political cultures will have lower percentages of women of color legislators.

Furthermore, states that are characterized as Traditionalistic are also states where we typically see higher levels of conservative political ideology. Squire confirms this finding for women—lower levels of female office holding in states with higher levels of conservative ideology.[64] But, he found the opposite for black office holding—higher percentages of black legislators in conservative states. Casellas found, however, that higher levels of liberal ideology among the state population significantly predicted where Latino legislators served.[65] However, neither of these studies focuses specifically on how ideology has an impact on women of color legislators. As such, and following the same reasoning from above in terms of the concentration of white women and women of color legislators, I believe my test will confirm the value of higher levels of liberal political ideologies in predicting where white women will serve, but that we will not see similar relationship for women of color legislators.

> H3a: States with higher levels of liberal political ideology will have higher percentages of female legislators.
>
> H3b: States with higher levels of liberal political ideology will have higher percentages of white female legislators.
>
> H3c: States with higher levels of liberal political ideology will have lower percentages of women of color legislators.

Relatedly, higher percentages of minority populations are concentrated in certain regions of the nation and map onto the pattern of minority office holding fairly well—where we see higher percentages of minority populations, we also see higher percentages of minority office holders.[66] My expectation is that higher percentages of minority populations will be positively and significantly related to office holding by women of color.[67] Clearly a substantial minority population is a necessary condition for electoral service, both in terms of how it affects the potential pool of candidates and with regard to the minority electorate's desire to elect "one of their own."[68] For white women legislators, I expect the relationship to be negative. What I suspect is that previous tests of the model may be capturing the legislative presence of women of color, and this particular variable may not have the same explanatory power within an intersectional framework.

> H4a: States with higher percentages of minority populations will have higher percentages of female legislators.
> H4b: States with higher percentages of minority populations will have lower percentages of white female legislators.
> H4c: States with higher percentages of minority populations will have higher percentages of women of color legislators.

The level of legislative professionalization presents a unique opportunity for applying an intersectional framework. The research that looks at how professionalization impacts women and minorities tends to find a negative relationship for women and positive relationship for minority office holding.[69] How professionalization relates to women of color legislators is not addressed. Thus, I rely on the logic presented in the women and politics literature, which assumes that more professionalized legislatures make office holding more appealing and, therefore, more competitive. Because female candidates may be less likely to run in these competitive environments, I speculate that professionalization will have a negative impact on the legislative service of both white women and women of color.[70]

> H5a: States with higher levels of legislative professionalization will have lower percentages of female legislators.

H5b: States with higher levels of legislative professionalization will have lower percentages of white female legislators

H5c: States with higher levels of legislative professionalization will have lower percentages of women of color legislators

The race and ethnic politics literature strongly suggests that I including a variable that accounts for the effects of the VRA. This is tricky, however, especially because the data I utilize for the other variables of in this project consist of aggregated state-level data. Other studies utilize district-level data, which are not comparable to a state-level study. As well, how this is measured varies a bit across studies. Some use multimember districts, others use the density of the minority population in a given state and/or district, one uses majority-minority districts, and another show how specific sections of the VRA affect particular districts.[71]

I could, for instance, create a dummy variable that indicates whether the state falls under VRA provisions. However, operationalizing the variable in that way correlates highly with political culture and percent of the minority population in the state. The same can be said regarding majority-minority districts. Also, neither of those measurements comports with my specific test derived from the women and politic literature, in which multimember districts are most commonly used.

The other possible method for capturing VRA effects would be to include a variable for multimember districts (MMDs). Clucas explains that "[m]uch of the scholarly interest in MMDs emerged in response to the demands placed on the states by the Voting Rights Act of 1965 for better representation of minority interests."[72] MMDs are traditionally associated with black vote dilution—single-member districts overcome this issue to a certain extent and are cited as being quite favorable for the election of candidates of color.[73] For example, Grofman and Handley explain that, in their analysis of some of the effects of the VRA in the South, "the number of black legislators increases as states [in the South] shift to single-member districts" from 1965 to 1985.[74]

Other scholars contend that the opposite is true for female representation—MMDs are favorable to the election of women whereas single-member districts are not.[75] In terms of the intersection of race and gender, most studies agree that MMDs are favorable for women but not for legislators of color.[76] For example, Rule documents that "[b]y analyzing Anglo and black women separately, we learn that multimember districts are best for both groups of women.[77] However, for black, Hispanic, and Anglo men, single-member districts are most favorable, while white women and women of color are more likely to be elected in multi-member districts." Darcy, Hadley, and Kirksey mirror Rule's findings and state that "[regardless of race, women fare better in multi-member district systems."[78]

Although not a perfect measure of VRA provisions, including a variable for multimember districts will partially capture some of its effects, and I expect that multimember districts will positively predict where both white women and women of color serve.

H6a: States with multimember districts will have higher percentages of female legislators.
H6b: States with multimember districts will have higher percentages of white female legislators.
H6c: States with multimember districts will have higher percentages of women of color legislators.

Taking all of the preceding into account, Table 2.1 provides a typology of the hypothesized conditions under which a state-level environment might be more, or less, "women-friendly" and indicates whether or not the same variable will equally predict the presence of white female and women of color legislators.[79] The goal here is to develop an intersectional framework for understanding the underlying conditions that are more or less conducive for predicting the electoral presence of women of color, as well as to highlight that these processes are not the same for white women.

This typology of intersectional representation at the state level echoes the women and politics literature as well as the race and ethnic politics literature reviewed in the above

Table 2.1 Intersectional Typology of Representation at the State Level: Will a State Have Higher Percentages of Women, White Women, and Women of Color Legislators?

Independent Variable	Women	White Women	Women of Color
Higher Percentages of Professional Women	Yes	Yes	Yes
Moralistic Political Culture	Yes	Yes	No
Higher Levels of Liberal Ideology	Yes	Yes	No
Higher Percentages of Minority Population	Yes	No	Yes
More Professionalized Legislature	No	No	No
Multimember Districts in the State	Yes	Yes	Yes

sections and incorporates the knowledge gained from both fields. In the words of Smooth, asserting predictions "at the intersection of race and gender politics makes conversations messy. It requires the interaction of two parallel yet divergent areas of scholarship and activism: race and politics and women and politics."[80] For this reason, and to the best extent possible, I have been careful to call upon the findings only derived from comparable studies across both literatures—those that assist in explaining the geographical variation in office holding, regressed against other factors, for both women and minority state legislators. If we put women of color legislators at the center of analysis, what can be said about the intersection of gender and race/ethnicity in terms of state legislative office holding? Does the conventional wisdom from both literatures apply to the case of women of color legislators? Does it help us to understand the smaller gender gap in office holding among legislators of color?

In Chapters 4 and 5, I test the preceding expectations and the typology by analyze data from a twenty-year time span (1990 to 2010) and assess whether this particular set of factors equally predict the presence of white women and women of color in U.S. state legislatures, as well as whether this same set of variables explain the smaller gender gap in office holding by legislators of color. But, first, in the next chapter, I illustrate the descriptive legislative landscape across the fifty states and more fully discuss the primary dependent variables of interest in this project. Where do we see higher percentages of women state legislators? Is this pattern the same for both white women and women of color? For comparability purposes, I match this racial/ethnic comparison with data on legislators of color across the states, disaggregated by gender. Where do we see higher percentages of legislators of color? Is this pattern the same for both women and men of color?

NOTES

1. Barbara Burrell, "Women Candidates in Open Seat Primaries for the U.S. House of Representatives, 1968–1990," *Legislative Studies Quarterly* 17, no. 4 (November 1992): 493–508; and Barbara Burrell, "Women's and Men's Campaigns for the U.S. House of Representatives, 1972–1982: A Finance Gap?" *American Politics Quarterly* (July 1985): 251–272.
2. Richard Fox, *Gender Dynamics in Congressional Elections* (Thousand Oaks, CA: Sage, 1997); Burrell, "Women's and Men's Campaigns"; Burrell, "Women Candidates in Open Seat Primaries"; Barbara Burrell, *A Woman's Place Is in the House: Campaigning for Congress in the Feminist Era* (Ann Arbor: University of Michigan Press, 1994); Barbara Burrell, "Campaign Finance: Women's Experience in the Modern Era" in *Women in Elected Office: Past, Present, and Future*, ed. Sue Thomas and Clyde Wilcox (New York: Oxford University Press, 1998): 26–37; Robert Darcy, Susan Welch, and Janet Clark, *Women, Elections, and Representation*, 2nd ed. (Lincoln: Nebraska University Press, 1994); Carole Jean Uhlaner and Kay Lehman Schlozman, "Candidate Gender and Congressional Campaign Receipts," *Journal of Politics* 48, no. 1 (2009): 30–50; and Susan J. Carroll, *Women as Candidates in American Politics*, 2nd ed. (Bloomington: Indiana University Press, 1994).
3. Jennifer L. Lawless and Richard L. Fox, *It Takes a Candidate: Why Women Don't Run for Office* (New York: Cambridge University Press, 2005); Jennifer Lawless and Richard Fox, *It Still Takes a Candidate: Why Women Don't Run for Office* (New York: Cambridge University Press, 2010); and Jennifer

Lawless, *Becoming a Candidate: Political Ambition and the Decision to Run for Office* (New York: Cambridge University Press, 2012).

4. Wilma Rule, "Why More Women Are State Legislators: A Research Note," *Western Political Quarterly* 43, no. 2 (1990): 432–448; Wilma Rule, "Why Are More Women State Legislators?" in *Women in Politics: Outsiders or Insiders?* 3rd ed., ed. Lois Duke Whitaker (Upper Saddle River, NJ: Prentice Hall, 1999): 190–201; John F. Camobreco and Michelle A. Barnello, "Postmaterialism and Post-Industrialism: Cultural Influences on Female Representation in State Legislatures," *State Politics and Policy Quarterly* 3, no. 2 (Summer 2003): 117–138; K. Sanbonmatsu, "Political Parties and the Recruitment of Women to State Legislatures," *Journal of Politics* 64, no. 3 (August 2002): 791–809; Kira Sanbonmatsu, *Where Women Run: Gender and Party in the American States* (Ann Arbor: University of Michigan Press, 2006); David B. Hill, "Political Culture and Female Political Representation," *The Journal of Politics* 43 (1981): 159–168; Carol Nechemias, "Changes in the Election of Women to U.S. State Legislative Seats," *Legislative Studies Quarterly* 8, no. 1 (1987): 125–142; Barbara Norrander and Clyde Wilcox, "The Geography of Gender Power: Women in State Legislatures," in *Women and Elective Office: Past, Present, and Future*, ed. Sue Thomas and Clyde Wilcox (New York: Oxford University Press, 1998): 103–117; Barbara Norrander and Clyde Wilcox, "Change in Continuity in the Geography of Women State Legislators," in *Women and Elective Office: Past, Present, and Future*, 2nd ed., ed. Sue Thomas and Clyde Wilcox (New York: Oxford University Press, 2005): 176–196; Kevin Arceneaux, "The 'Gender Gap' in State Legislative Representation: New Data to Tackle and Old Question," *Political Research Quarterly* 54 (2001): 143–160; and Robert E. Hogan, "The Influences of State and District Conditions on the Representation of Women in U.S. State Legislatures," *American Politics Research* 29 (2001): 4–24.

5. Of course, there is a robust discussion within the comparative women and politics literature on the cross-national variation in female office holding. There, a supply and demand model is most commonly used to explain the variation in women's political office holding across nations. See, for example, Miki Caul Kittilson, *Challenging Parties, Changing Parliaments: Women and Elected Office in Contemporary Western Europe* (Columbus, OH: Ohio State University Press, 2006); Mona Lena Krook, "Beyond Supply and Demand: A Feminist-Institutionalist Theory of Candidate Selection," *Political Research Quarterly* 63, no. 4 (2010): 707–720; and Yvonne

Galligan, Sara Clavero, and Marina Calloni, *Gender Politics and Democracy in Post-Socialist Europe* (Farmington Hills, MI: Barbara Budrich Publishers, 2007). Supply indicators are "identified as inhibiting the pool of eligible female aspirants" and mainly revolve around gender socialization and political ambition. The demand side consists of aggregate, institutional-level structures such as culture, political parties, and quota systems. See Galligan, Clavero, and Calloni, *Gender Politics and Democracy*, 96.
6. Barbara Palmer and Dennis Simon, *Breaking the Political Glass Ceiling: Women and Congressional Elections*, 2nd ed. (New York: Routledge, 2008), 181.
7. Hill, "Political Culture," 167
8. Nechemias, "Changes in the Election of Women," 128.
9. Rule, "Why More Women Are State Legislators"; and Rule, "Why Are More Women State Legislators?"
10. Norrander and Wilcox, "The Geography of Gender Power."
11. Ibid., 114–115.
12. Hogan, "The Influences of State and District Conditions."
13. Arceneaux, "The 'Gender Gap.'"
14. See, Hill, "Political Culture"; Nechemias, "Changes in the Election of Women"; Rule, "Why More Women Are State Legislators"; Rule, "Why Are More Women State Legislators?"; Norrander and Wilcox, "The Geography of Gender Power"; Hogan, "The Influences of State and District Conditions"; Arceneaux, "The 'Gender Gap'"; Sanbonmatsu, "Political Parties and the Recruitment"; and Lawless and Fox, *It Takes a Candidate*.

Also, studies of political participation at the mass level have illustrated that socioeconomic status (SES) is one of the best predictors of political engagement. See Sidney Verba, Kay Lehman Schlozman, Henry Brady, *Voice and Equality: Civic Voluntarism in American Politics* (Cambridge, MA: Harvard University Press, 1995). Likewise, those who are embedded within active civic networks are more likely to participate, to be recruited to participate, and to have the necessary skills to feel efficacious about their participation. See Verba, Schlozman, and Brady, *Voice and Equality*.
15. Hill, "Political Culture"; Nechemias, "Changes in the Election of Women"; Norrander and Wilcox, "The Geography of Gender Power"; Norrander and Wilcox, "Change in Continuity"; Hogan, "The Influences of State and District Conditions"; and Arceneaux, "The 'Gender Gap.'"
16. E.J. Barrett, "The Policy Priorities of African-American Women In State Legislatures," *Legislative Studies Quarterly* 20, no. 2 (May 1995): 223–247; Sanbonmatsu, "Political Parties"; Arceneaux, "The 'Gender Gap'"; Nechemias, "Changes

in the Election of Women"; Rule, "Why More Women Are State Legislators"; Rule, "Why Are More Women State Legislators?"; Norrander and Wilcox, "The Geography of Gender Power"; Hogan, "The Influences of State and District Conditions"; and Zoe M. Oxley and Richard L. Fox, "Women in Executive Office: Variation across American States," *Political Research Quarterly* 57, no. 1 (March 2004): 113–120.

17. Elazar classifies the states into three general categories that follow a loose continuum from Traditionalistic to Individualistic to Moralistic, with some states categorized as a mixture of two. Traditionalistic states have an electorate "that accepts a substantially hierarchical society as part of the ordered nature of things . . . [and] tries to limit [the role of government] to securing the continued maintenance of the existing social order." Individualistic states are defined as those that "emphasizes the centrality of private concerns, [and] it places a premium on limiting community intervention . . . into private activities." Moralistic states place primary value on "politics as a public activity centered on some notion of the public good and properly devoted to the advancement of the public interest." See Daniel J. Elazar, *American Federalism: A View from the States* (New York: Thomas Y. Crowell Company, 1966), 79, 86–87, 90, 93.
18. Hill, "Political Culture"; Nechemias, "Changes in the Election of Women"; Rule, "Why More Women Are State Legislators"; Wilma Rule, "Why Are More Women State Legislators?"; Norrander and Wilcox, "The Geography of Gender Power"; Hogan, "The Influences of State and District Conditions"; and Arceneaux, "The 'Gender Gap.'"
19. Norrander and Wilcox, "The Geography of Gender Power"; Norrander and Wilcox, "Change in Continuity"; Arceneaux, "The 'Gender Gap'"; and Hogan, "The Influences of State and District Conditions."
20. Hogan, "The Influences of State and District Conditions."
21. Norrander and Wilcox, "The Geography of Gender Power"; Norrander and Wilcox, "Change in Continuity"; Arceneaux, "The 'Gender Gap'"; and Hogan, "The Influences of State and District Conditions."
22. Hill, "Political Culture"; Hogan, "The Influences of State and District Conditions"; Arceneaux, "The 'Gender Gap.'"
23. Hill, "Political Culture"; Nechemias, "Changes in the Election of Women"; Arceneaux, "The 'Gender Gap'"; and Hogan, "The Influences of State and District Conditions."
24. Kimberle Crenshaw, "Demarginalizing the Intersection of Race and Sex: A Black Feminist Critique of Antidiscrimination Doctrine, Feminist Theory and Antiracist Politics," *University of Chicago Legal Forum* (1989): 139–167; Kimberle

Crenshaw, "Mapping the Margins: Intersectionality, Identity Politics, and Violence Against Women of Color," *Stanford Law Review* 43, no. 6 (July 1991): 1241–1299; Jane Mansbridge and Katherine Tate, "Race Trumps Gender: The Thomas Nomination in the Black Community," *PS: Political Science & Politics* 25, no. 3 (1992): 488–92; Claudine Gay and Katherine Tate, "Doubly Bound: The Impact of Gender and Race on the Politics of Black Women," *Political Psychology* 19, no. 1 (1998): 169–184; Mary Hawkesworth, "Congressional Enactments of Race-Gender: Toward a Theory of Raced-Gendered Institutions," *American Political Science Review* 97, no. 4 (November 2003): 529–550.

25. Mansbridge and Tate, "Race Trumps Gender," 488.
26. Gary Moncrief, Joel Thompson, and Robert Schuhmann, "Gender, Race, and the State Legislature: A Research Note on the Double Disadvantage Hypothesis," *Social Science Journal* 28 (1991): 481–87; Jewel L. Prestage, "In Quest of African American Political Woman," *Annals of the American Academy of Political and Social Science* 515 (May 1991): 88–103; Marsha J. Darling, "African-American Women in State Elective Office in the South," in *Women and Elective Office: Past, Present and Future*, edited by Sue Thomas and Clyde Wilcox (New York: New York University Press, 1998), 150–162; Linda Faye Williams, "The Civil Rights-Black Power Legacy: Black Women Elected Officials at the Local, State, and National Levels," in *Sisters in the Struggle: African American Women in the Civil Rights-Black Power Movement*, ed. Bettye Collier-Thomas and V.P. Franklin (New York: New York University Press, 2001), 306–331; Pei-te Lien, Carol Hardy-Fanta, Dianne M. Pinderhughes, and Christine Marie Sierra, "Expanding Categorization at the Intersection of Race and Gender: 'Women of Color' as a Political Category for African American, Latina, Asian American, and American Indian Women" (paper presented at the Annual Meeting of the American Political Science Association, Boston, August 27–31, 2007); Luis Ricardo Fraga, Linda Lopez, Valerie Martinez-Ebers, and Ricardo Ramirez, "Gender and Ethnicity: Patterns of Electoral Success and Legislative Advocacy Among Latina and Latino State Officials in Four States," *Journal of Women, Politics and Policy* 28, no. 3–4 (2006): 122–145; Robert Darcy and Charles D. Hadley, "Black Women in Politics: The Puzzle Of Success," *Social Science Quarterly* 69, no. 3 (September 1988): 629–645; Gay and Tate, "Doubly Bound"; and Tasha S. Philpot and Hanes Walton Jr., "One of Our Own: Black Female Candidates and the Voters Who Support Them," *American Journal of Political Science* 51, no. 1 (2007): 49–62.

27. Todd Collins and Laura Moyer, "Gender, Race, and Intersectionality on the Federal Appellate Bench," *Political Research Quarterly* 61, no. 2 (June 2008): 219–227; Diane-Michele Prindeville and Teresa Braley Gomez, "American Indian Women Leaders, Public Policy, and the Importance of Gender and Ethnic Identity," *Women and Politics* 20, no. 2 (1991): 17–32; Wendy Smooth, "African American Women State Legislators: The Impact of Gender and Race on Legislative Influence" (PhD diss., University of Maryland College Park, 2001); Luis Ricardo Fraga, Valerie Martinez-Ebers, Linda Lopez, and Ricardo Ramirez, "Strategic Intersectionality: Gender, Ethnicity, and Political Incorporation" (paper delivered at the *Western Political Science Association's* annual meeting, Oakland, CA., March 17–19, 2005); and Byron D. Orey and Wendy Smooth, with Kimberly S. Adams and Kisha H. Clark, "Race and Gender Matter: Refining Models of Legislative Policy Making in State Legislatures," *Journal of Women, Politics & Policy* 28, no. 314 (2006) 97–119.
28. Wendy Smooth, "Intersectionality in Electoral Politics: A Mess Worth Making," *Politics & Gender* 2, no. 3 (2006), 400–414.
29. Hawkesworth, "Congressional Enactments of Race-Gender," 530.
30. Palmer and Simon, *Breaking the Political Glass Ceiling*; and Barbara Palmer and Dennis Simon, *Women and Congressional Elections: A Century of Change* (Boulder, CO: Lynne Rienner Publishers, 2012).
31. Palmer and Simon, *Breaking the Political Glass Ceiling*.
32. Palmer and Simon, *Women and Congressional Elections*, 209.
33. Ibid.
34. Stanley Caress, "The Influence of Term Limits on the Electoral Success of Women," *Women and Politics* 20, no. 3 (1999): 45–63; Susan J. Carroll and Krista Jenkins, "Do Term Limits Help Women Get Elected?" *Social Science Quarterly* 82, no. 1 (March 2001): 197–201; and Susan J. Carroll and Krista Jenkins, "Unrealized Opportunity? Term Limits and the Representation of Women in State Legislatures," *Women and Politics* 23, no. 4 (2001): 1–30.
35. Susan J. Carroll and Krista Jenkins, "Increasing Diversity or More of the Same? Term Limits and the Representation of Women, Minorities, and Minority Women in State Legislatures" (paper presented at the American Political Science Association's annual meeting, San Francisco, August 30–September 2, 2001), 8.
36. Ibid.

37. Katie E. Ostrander and Pei-te Lien, "Structural and Contextual Factors in the Election of Women and Minorities to Sub-National Offices: A Review of the Literature" (paper presented at the Annual Meeting of the Western Political Science Association, San Francisco, April 1–3, 2010); Cathy J. Cohen, "A Portrait of Marginality: The Study of Women of Color in American Politics," In *Women and American Politics: New Questions, New Directions*, ed. Susan J. Carroll (Oxford: Oxford University Press, 2003), 190–213; Edith J. Barrett, "Black Women in State Legislatures: The Relationship of Race and Gender to the Legislative Experience," in *The Impact of Women in Public Office*, ed. Susan J. Carroll (Bloomington: Indiana University Press, 2001), 185–204; and Lisa J. Montoya, Carol Hardy-Fanta, and Sonia Garcia, "Latina Politics: Gender, Participation, and Leadership," *PS: Political Science and Politics* 33, no. 3 (September 2000), 555–561.
38. Anne Marie Cammisa and Beth Reingold, "Women in State Legislatures and State Legislative Research: Beyond Sameness and Difference," *State Politics and Policy Quarterly* 4, no. 2 (Summer 2004): 185, 202.
39. Ostrander and Lien, "Structural and Contextual Factors," 2.
40. Katherine Tate, "African American Female Senatorial Candidates: Twin Assets or Double Liabilities?," in *African American Power and Politics: The Political Context Variable*, ed. Hanes Walton Jr. (New York: Columbia University Press, 1997), 264–281; Darling, "African-American Women in State Elective Office"; Marianne Githens and Jewel L. Prestage, *A Portrait of Marginality: The Political Behavior of the American Woman* (New York: David McKay Company, Inc, 1977); Herrington J. Bryce and Alan E. Warrick, "Black Women in Electoral Politics," in *A Portrait of Marginality: The Political Behavior of the American Woman*, ed. M. Githens and J.L. Prestage (New York: David McKay, 1977) 395–400; Paule Cruz Takash, "Breaking Barriers to Representation: Chicana/Latina Elected Officials in California" in *Women Transforming Politics: An Alternative Reader*, ed. Cathy J. Cohen, Kathleen B. Jones, and Joan C. Tronto (New York: New York University Press, 1997), 412–434; Montoya, Hardy-Fanta, and Garcia, "Latina Politics"; Williams, "The Civil Rights-Black Power Legacy"; Carol Hardy-Fanta, Christine M. Sierra, Pei-te Lien, Dianne M. Pinderhughes, and Wartnya L. Davis, "Race, Gender, and Descriptive Representation: An Exploratory View of Multicultural Elected Leadership in the United States" (paper delivered at the American Political Science Association's annual meeting, Washington, DC,

September 1–5, 2005); Evelyn Simien, *Black Feminist Voices in Politics* (Albany: State University of New York Press, 2006); Philpot and Walton, "One of Our Own"; Jane Junn, "Assimilating or Coloring Participation? Gender, Race, and Democratic Political Participation," in *Women Transforming Politics: An Alternative Reader*, ed. Cathy J. Cohen, Kathleen B. Jones, and Joan C. Tronto (New York: New York University Press, 1997), 387–397; Prestage, "Black Women State Legislators"; Carol Hardy-Fanta, *Latina Politics, Latino Politics: Gender, Culture, and Political Participation in Boston* (Philadelphia: Temple University Press, 1993); Mary S. Pardo, *Mexican American Women Activists: Identity and Resistance in Two Los Angeles Communities* (Philadelphia: Temple University Press, 1998); and Sonia R. Garcia and Marisela Marquez, "Motivational and Attitudinal Factors Amongst Latinas in U.S. Electoral Politics," *NWSA Journal* 13, no. 2 (Summer 2001): 112–122.

41. Darling, "African-American Women"; Barrett, "Black Women in State Legislatures"; Diane Prindeville, "Feminist Nations? A Study of Native American Women in Southwestern Tribal Politics," *Political Research Quarterly* 57, no. 1 (2004): 101–112; Prindeville and Gomez, "American Indian Women Leaders"; Kathleen A. Bratton, Kerry L. Haynie, and Beth Reingold, "Agenda Setting and African American Women in State Legislatures" (paper presented at the Annual Meeting of the American Political Science Association, Washington, DC, September 1–4, 2005); Fraga et al., "Strategic Intersectionality"; Fraga et al., "Gender and Ethnicity: Patterns of Electoral Success"; Wendy Smooth, "African American Women State Legislators: The Impact of Gender and Race on Legislative Influence." (PhD diss., University of Maryland College Park, 2001); Williams, "The Civil Rights-Black Power Legacy"; Jerry Perkins, "Political Ambition among Black and White Women: An Intragender Test of the Socialization Model," *Women & Politics* 6, no. 1 (Spring 1986): 27–40; R. A. Clawson and J. A. Clark, "The Attitudinal Structure of African American Women Party Activists: The Impact of Race, Gender and Religion," *Political Research Quarterly* 56, no. 2 (2003): 211–21; Pei-te Lien, Dianne M. Pinderhughes, Carol Hardy-Fanta, and Christine Marie Sierra, "The Voting Rights Act and the Election of Nonwhite Officials," *PS: Political Science & Politics* 40, no. 3 (2007): 489–94; Angela Frederick, "Bringing Narrative In: Race-Gender Storytelling, Political Ambition, and Women's Path to Public Office," *Journal of Women, Politics & Policy* 34, no. 2 (2013): 113–137; and Robert Moore, "Religion, Race, and Gender Differences in Political Ambition," *Politics & Gender* 1, no. 4 (2005): 577–596.

42. Smooth, "Intersectionality in Electoral Politics."
43. Prestage, "In Quest of African American Political Woman"; Darcy and Hadley, "Black Women in Politics"; Pachon and DeSipio, "Latino Elected Officials"; Darcy, Welch, and Clark, *Women, Elections, and Representation*; Takash, "Breaking Barriers to Representation"; Montoya, Hardy-Fanta, and Garcia, "Latina Politics"; Fraga et al., "Gender and Ethnicity"; Katherine Tate, *Black Faces in the Mirror: African Americans and Their Representatives in the U.S. Congress* (Chicago: University of Chicago Press, 2003); Pei-te et al., "The Voting Rights Act"; Williams, "The Civil Rights-Black Power Legacy"; Darcy and Hadley, "Black Women in Politics"; Moncrief, Thompson, and Schuhmann, "Gender, Race, and the State Legislature"; E.J. Barrett, "Policy Priorities."
44. Darcy and Hadley, "Black Women in Politics," 642.
45. Moncrief, Thompson, and Schuhmann, "Gender, Race, and the State Legislature."
46. Fraga et al., "Gender and Ethnicity," 122–123.
47. Ibid., 123.
48. Ibid., 131.
49. But see Karnig and Welch who contend that women of color at the local level experience "double jeopardy." In their study of municipal-level offices, they note "the inability of black women to benefit from the factors which favorably influence the representation of black men." See Albert K. Karing and Susan Welch, "Sex and Ethnic Differences in Municipal Representation," *Social Science Quarterly* 60, no. 3 (December 1979): 470, 479.
50. Darcy and Hadley, "Black Women in Politics"; Moncrief, Thompson, and Schuhmann, "Gender, Race, and the State Legislature"; and Fraga et al., "Gender and Ethnicity: Patterns of Electoral Success".
51. Kathleen A. Bratton, "The Behavior and Success of Latino Legislators: Evidence from the States," *Social Science Quarterly* 87, no. 5 (Dec 2006): 1136–1157; Charles E. Menifeld, Ed., *Representation of Minority Groups in the U.S.: Implications for the Twenty-First Century* (Lanham, MD: Austin and Winfield Publishers, 2001); Walter Clark Wilson, "Latino Congressional Staffers and Policy Responsiveness: An Analysis of Latino Interest Agenda Setting," *Politics, Groups, and Identities* 1, no. 2 (2013), 164–180; Christian R. Grose, *Congress in Black and White: Race and Representation in Washington and at Home* (New York: Cambridge University Press, 2011); Katherine Tate, *Black Faces in the Mirror: African Americans and Their Representatives in the U.S. Congress* (Chicago: University of Chicago Press, 2003); Carol M. Swain, *Black Faces, Black Interests: The Representation of African Americans in Congress* (Cambridge, MA: Harvard University Press, 1995);

David Lublin, *The Paradox of Representation: Racial Gerrymandering and Minority Interests in Congress* (Princeton, NJ: Princeton University Press, 1997); Susan Welch and John R. Hibbing, "Hispanic Representation in the U.S. Congress," *Social Science Quarterly* 65, no. 2 (June 1984): 328–335; David T. Canon, *Race, Redistricting, and Representation: The Unintended Consequences of Black Majority Districts* (Chicago: University of Chicago Press, 1999); Gary M. Segura and Shaun Bowler, *Diversity in Democracy: Minority Representation in the United States* (Charlottesville, VA: University of Virginia Press, 2005); Kerry Haynie, *African American State Legislators in the American States* (New York: Columbia University Press, 2001); Jason Casellas, *Latino Representation in State Houses and Congress* (Cambridge: Cambridge University Press, 2011); Katrina L. Gamble, "Black Political Representation: An Examination of Legislative Activity Within U.S. House Committees," *Legislative Studies Quarterly* 32, no. 3 (August 2007): 421–447; Kenny J. Whitby, *The Color of Representation: Congressional Behavior and Black Interests* (Ann Arbor: University of Michigan Press, 1997); Michael D. Minta, *Oversight: Representing the Interest of Blacks and Latinos in Congress* (Princeton, NJ: Princeton University Press, 2011), David Hedge, James Button, and Mary Spear, "Accounting for the Quality of Black Legislative Life: The View from the States," *American Journal of Political Science* 40, no. 1 (1996): 82–98, Richard Fenno, *Going Home: Black Representatives and Their Constituents* (Chicago: University of Chicago Press, 2003); and Chris T. Owens, "Black Substantive Representation in State Legislatures from 1971–1994," *Social Science Quarterly* 86, no. 4 (Dec. 2005): 779–791.

52. Minta, *Oversight*, 542.
53. Smooth, "African American Women State Legislators"; Fraga et al., "Gender and Ethnicity: Patterns of Electoral Success"; Kathleen A. Bratton and Kerry L. Haynie, "Agenda Setting and Legislative Success in State Legislatures: The Effects of Gender and Race," *The Journal of Politics* 61, no. 3 (1999): 658–679; and Bratton, Haynie, and Reingold, "Agenda Setting."
54. Jason P. Casellas, "The Institutional and Demographic Determinants of Latino Representation," *Legislative Studies Quarterly* 34, no. 3 (August 2009): 399–425; Casellas, *Latino Representation*; Haynie, *African American State Legislators*; and Lien et al., "The Voting Rights Act.".
55. Lien et al., "The Voting Rights Act," 491–492.
56. Although, Geron and Lai indicate that this is not necessarily the case for Asian American elected officials in the mainland United States and Lien et al. "find that only Black legislators are elected mostly from districts in which the majority of the

population is of the same race." See Kim Geron and James S. Lai, "Beyond Symbolic Representation: A Comparison of the Electoral Pathways and Policy Priorities of Asian American and Latino Elected Officials," *Asian Law Journal* 9 (May 2002): 41–81; Lien et al., "The Voting Rights Act," 491; Thomas E. Cavanagh and Denise Stockton, *Black Elected Officials and Their Constituencies* (Washington, DC: Joint Center for Political Studies, 1983); Bernard Grofman and Lisa Handley, "Black Representation: Making Sense of Electoral Geography at Different Levels of Government," *Legislative Studies Quarterly* 14, no. 2 (May 1989): 265–279; Bernard Grofman and Lisa Handley, "Minority Population Proportion and Black and Hispanic Congressional Success in the 1970s and 1980s," *American Politics Quarterly* 17, no. 4 (October 1989): 436–445; Welch and Hibbing, "Hispanic Representation"; Charles S. Bullock, "The Election of Blacks in the South: Preconditions and Consequences," *American Journal of Political Science* 19, no. 4 (November 1975): 727–739; and James S. Lai, Wendy K. Tam Cho, Thomas P. Kim, and Okiyoshi Takeda, "Asian Pacific-American Campaigns, Elections, and Elected Officials," *PS: Political Science and Politics* 34, no. 3 (September 2001): 611–617.
57. Cavanagh and Stockton, *Black Elected Officials*.
58. Casellas, *Latino Representation*.
59. Ibid., 45.
60. Barrett, "The Policy Priorities," 236.
61. Tate, *Black Faces in the Mirror*; Smooth, "Intersectionality"; and Smooth, "African American Women and Electoral Politics."
62. For example, Stephen Eisele states that "[t]o a large extent, recent gains in women's office holding have been fueled by the achievements of women of color candidates." See Stephen Eisele, "Women of Color in American Politics," published online at the Hunt Alternative's Political Parity Project, 2012, (http://www.politicalparity.org/page 1). Also see Darcy and Hadley, "Black Women in Politics"; Fraga et al., "Gender and Ethnicity: Patterns of Electoral Success"; and Smooth, "Intersectionality."
63. Williams, "The Civil Rights-Black Power Legacy"; Prestage, "Black Women State Legislators"; Darcy and Hadley, "Black Women in Politics"; and Moncrief, Thompson, and Schuhmann, "Gender, Race, and the State Legislature."
64. Peverill Squire, "Legislative Professionalization and Membership Diversity in State Legislatures," *Legislative Studies Quarterly* 17, no. 1 (February 1992): 69–79.
65. Casellas, "The Institutional and Demographic Determinants"; and Casellas, *Latino Representation*.

66. Although this relationship is not perfect, and I offer a more nuanced discussion of this particular correlation in Chapter 3.
67. Peverill Squire, "Legislative Professionalization"; Barrett, "Policy Priorities"; Rodney E. Hero, *Faces of Inequality: Social Diversity in American Politics* (New York: Oxford University Press, 1998); Hogan, "The Influences of State and District Conditions"; and Fraga et al., "Gender and Ethnicity: Patterns of Electoral Success."
68. Philpot and Walton, "One of Our Own."
69. See Peverill Squire, "Legislative Professionalization"; Hero, *Faces of Inequality*; and Casellas, *Latino Representation*. However, Casellas finds that this significantly predicts Latino state legislative service only when it interacts with the percentage of Latino citizens in the state. See Casellas, "The Institutional and Demographic Determinants"; and Casellas, *Latino Representation*.
70. Lawless and Fox, *It Takes a Candidate*.
71. Elisabeth R. Gerber, Rebecca B. Morton, and Thomas A. Rietz, "Minority Representation in Multimember Districts," *American Political Science Review* 92, no. 1 (March 1998): 127–144; Bernard Grofman and Lisa Handley, "The Impact of the Voting Rights Act on Black Representation in Southern State Legislatures," *Legislative Studies Quarterly* 16, no. 1 (February 1991): 111–128; Cavanagh and Stockton, *Black Elected Officials*; Grofman and Handley, "Black Representation"; Grofman and Handley, "Minority Population Proportion"; Casellas, "The Institutional and Demographic Determinants"; Casellas, *Latino Representation*; Lai et al., "Asian Pacific-American Campaigns,"; and Lien et al., "The Voting Rights Act."
72. Richard A. Clucas, "Improving the Harvest of State Legislative Research," *State Politics and Policy Quarterly* 3, no. 4 (Winter 2003): 392.
73. Grofman and Handley, "The Impact of the Voting Rights Act."
74. Ibid., 112.
75. Norrander and Wilcox, "Change in Continuity"; Rule, "Why More Women Are State Legislators"; Arceneaux, "The 'Gender Gap' "; Albert Nelson, *Emerging Influentials in State Legislatures: Women, Blacks, and Hispanics* (Westport, CT: Praeger, 1991); Richard E. Matland and Deborah Dwight Brown, "District Magnitude's Effect on Female Representation in U.S. State Legislatures," *Legislative Studies Quarterly* 17, no. 4 (November 1992): 469–492; and James D. King, "Single-Member Districts and the Representation of Women in American State Legislatures: The Effects of Electoral

System Change," *State Politics and Policy Quarterly* 2, no. 2 (Summer 2002): 161–175.
76. Robert Darcy, Charles D. Hadley, and Jason F. Kirksey, "Election Systems and the Representation of Black Women in American State Legislatures," *Women & Politics* 13, no. 2 (1993): 73–89; Grofman and Handley, "The Impact of the Voting Rights Act"; Gary F. Moncrief and Joel A. Thompson, "Electoral Structures and State Legislative Representation: A Research Note," *Journal of Politics* 54, no. 1 (February 1992): 246–256; and Wilma Rule, "Multimember Legislative Districts: Minority and Anglo Women's and Men's Recruitment Opportunity," in *United States Electoral Systems: Their Impact on Women and Minorities*, ed. Wilma Rule and Joseph F. Zimmerman (Westport, CT: Praeger, 1992), 57–72.
77. Rule, "Multimember Legislative Districts."
78. Darcy, Hadley, and Kirksey, "Election Systems," 85.
79. Palmer and Simon coined this term for women's legislative service at the congressional level. They found that certain districts with particular characteristics were more "women-friendly" than others. See Palmer and Simon, *Breaking the Political Glass Ceiling*; and Barbara Palmer and Dennis Simon, *Women and Congressional Elections: A Century of Change* (Boulder, CO: Lynne Rienner Publishers, 2012).
80. Smooth, "Intersectionality," 401.

3 Mapping the Terrain
Descriptive Representation at the Intersection of Gender and Race/Ethnicity

In 1990, two years before the "Year of the Woman" was heralded as a new age for women in politics, women represented 17.1% of all state legislators across the nation.[1] By 2010, 24.5% of all state legislators were women.[2] Although the descriptive representation of women did indeed increase over this twenty-year period, the aggregate percentages veil a more complex picture of women's legislative service. One such complexity is the variation we see in the percentage of female office holding across states. For example, in 2010, 38% of Colorado's legislature was composed of women, whereas South Carolina's consisted of only 10%. Again, this is not a new trend—we have consistently witnessed a range in female state legislative office holding across the states for the last four decades.[3]

Over this same period, the presence of women of color in state legislatures increased from 1.8% in 1990 to 4.8% in 2010, with Native American women serving in as few as seven legislatures to black women serving in as many as thirty-eight state legislatures.[4] We also saw a variation in their office holding across the states in 2010. No women of color served in four states, but in Hawaii, 28.9% of all state legislators were women of color. As briefly discussed in Chapter 1, although women of color are still underrepresented in terms of their population, they hold a higher racial/ethnic proportional share of legislative seat when compared to white women. Is this the case in all states? And what accounts for this higher comparative rate of office holding?

This chapter presents a descriptive overview of the five dependent variables utilized in this book and maps out the legislative service of women, white women, and women of color since 1990. For comparative purposes, I also provide data on legislators of color and men of color legislators. The data were collected for five points in time (1990, 1995, 2000, 2005, and 2010) by consulting several sources of published and non-published information. It is reported as the pooled average percentage of those time points within the total legislative body of for each group.[5] The first part of this chapter offers a note on the data collected and utilized for the dependent variables within the book. I account for how the data were gathered and compiled, as well as some of the obstacles I encountered as I went about this process. Also offered in this section is an explanation for how and why I employ the classification "women of color" as opposed to separate variables for each racial/ethnic group of women along with a few caveats about how the data should be interpreted.

The section after that provides a ranked list of the top ten and bottom ten states for women's legislative office holding and then breaks this down by white women and women of color legislators. What are the best- and worst-case scenarios? Where are women, white women, and women of color doing better? Where are they doing worse? Where we see higher percentages of women, do we also see higher percentages of women of color? Where we see higher percentages of legislators of color, do we see higher percentages of women of color? In other words, is the pattern more attributable to gender, race, or both?

Then, in keeping with the two research questions of interest, the next part of the chapter discusses what the geographical variation in office holding has looked like across the fifty states and document which states have demonstrated an increase and/or decrease in women's office holding. Which group of women has gained representation, and which group of women has lost representation? Is it the same pattern for all women? I do the same type of descriptive analysis for legislators of color disaggregated by gender. Afterward, I examine the gender gap and if it has increased or decreased since 1990 for women, white women, and women of color. Here, I also list state-level percentages. How has the gender gap in office holding increased or decreased over time and where? For which group of women under investigation?

By examining the pattern of representation for the last twenty years, three things become clear. First, legislative service by women of color is not equally distributed across the states. They tend to serve in particular states and regions, which is only partially attributable to the percentage of the minority population within the state.[6] Second, the pattern of descriptive representation by women of color does not fully mirror women *or* minority office holding. Where they serve is not predicted simply by looking at the gender or race/ethnicity composition of the state legislatures. Third, examining the gender gap in office holding by race/ethnicity reiterates these sentiments. The states with the highest and lowest white gender gaps in office holding do not match up with the legislator of color gender gap. Although there is some overlap, the majority of the top and bottom ten gender gap states are not the same for white women and women of color legislators.

A NOTE ON THE DATA

Two things should be noted about the dependent variable data presented in this chapter and the next. First, those who study politics at the intersection of race and gender will understand that collecting data on the gender and the race/ethnicity of legislators at the state level is an inherently difficult task. Multiplying that task by five time points produces an even more challenging undertaking. First, no one source houses all the data. I consulted five research centers, as well as several directories in order to locate the correct records for each year. On request, the Center for American Women and Politics (CAWP) and the National Association of Latino Elected Officials (NALEO) provided records for all five points in time in electronic format. CAWP compiled data for all female legislators by race/ethnicity, and NALEO did the same for all Latino legislators by gender. I utilized the *National Asian Pacific American Political Almanac* published by UCLA's Asian American Studies and Asian Pacific American Institute for Congressional Studies for data on Asian American legislators by gender.[7]

I had the most difficulty collecting data on black male and Native American male legislators. CAWP had provided black female and Native American female data, but no *consistently* published sources provide data on black or Native American legislators that is also easily accessible. After several attempts to contact both the National Black Caucus of State Legislators and the Joint Center, I finally got in touch with an incredibly helpful research analyst at the Joint Center, who provided the information on black legislators that I needed. The data for Native Americans were almost nonexistent. The National Conference of State Legislators (NCSL), which produces lists of legislators based on race and gender its website (but not consistently) for select points in time, had sporadic lists of Native American legislators. Contacting them directly helped to fill in the gaps for the Native American males identified in this data set.

Once this was accomplished, I matched up the relevant data to confirm the accuracy of the records. At this point in the collection process, there were ambiguities that needed to be resolved. For example, data on the race/ethnicity of all female legislators for each of the five time points were secured from CAWP, and data on the gender of all Latino legislators were gathered from NALEO. But then I had to make sure that the Latinas who were identified by CAWP also matched the same number of Latinas that NALEO had identified. If there was a discrepancy in the data, I had to consult other sources for verification (NCSL, state legislative websites, rosters, and the like). In cases of discrepancies, I erred on the side of two source confirmations. I am fairly confident that the resulting data on the gender and race/ethnicity legislators are accurate and complete to the best of my ability.

Second, aside from the challenges in compiling the data, it is important to note that the dependent variable for legislators of color, men of color, and women of color combines all racial/ethnic groups. Undoubtedly, combining all minority women might obscure what is truly going on. Separate models for black, Latino, Asian American, and American Indians would provide a richer story of how race intersects with office holding and better inform us about the nuances and differences that exist among racial and ethnic groups of women. Indeed, Lien et al. "caution against lumping together all women (and men) of color elected officials as one political category."[8] Although these authors note that there are differences among women of color along a variety of factors, they also find some areas of cohesion.[9] In another study, Hardy-Fanta et al. find that "there is evidence that commonality implied by the term 'women of color' has empirical support."[10]

Furthermore, there is some precedent for using the term *women of color* and for collapsing data. Hawkesworth invokes this term in her study of congressional women of color and combines the data she gathered for African American, Latina, and Asian American women.[11] Hawkesworth's reason for doing so is the same as mine: the "small n."[12] Grofman and Handley collapsed "minority (black plus Hispanic) population as a predictor of minority electoral success."[13]

Although this justification may not be wholly satisfying (for the reader or the author), collapsing the data was necessary in order to have a sufficient number of cases to test the model and will offer a broad base from which to then create more in-depth studies in the future.

In short, does combining all women of color conceal differences among racial/ethnic groups of women? Of course it does. But, if what other scholars have said about the women and politics literature is true, that what we know is primarily about white women, then the current study offers, at the very least, some insight into whether one aspect of our conventional wisdom applies to women of color, broadly conceived. The reader is advised to keep this in mind with respect to the results presented in this book. The main idea is to disaggregate gender by race/ethnicity in order to make a few observations about how each informs our understanding of the representational patterns of women of color legislators.

RANKING THE STATES

A January 2013 *New York Times* article by Katharine Q. Seelye declared "From Congress to Halls of State, in New

Hampshire, Women Rule." The article itself details the historic nature of the November 2012 elections, when New Hampshire "be[came] the first state in the nation's history to send an all-female delegation to Washington."[14] This phenomenon was not specific to women at the congressional level. Even at the state level, "women have long held prominent positions in New Hampshire government." Undeniably, New Hampshire has a stellar record in terms of electing women to their state legislature. The CAWP documents that New Hampshire has ranked within the top ten states for women's state legislative office holding several years, if not decades, running. What the article does not discuss is that these women are almost exclusively white.

Is this the case for all the states with higher levels of female state legislators? Table 3.1 lists the top ten and bottom ten states for women, white women, and women of color by using the pooled average of the percentage of their representational proportions for the five time points listed earlier.

By looking at the average percentage of females in the top ten states, it is clear that women are more likely to serve in northeastern and western states, with Maryland as the one southern outlier. The bottom ten states are all southern with the exception of Pennsylvania. However, where we see low percentages of women of color we do not necessarily see low proportions of white women. For example, the bottom ten states for women of color are mainly northeastern and midwestern states, with West Virginia and Kentucky as the exceptions, whereas the bottom ten states for white women are highly skewed toward southern states, with Pennsylvania and Hawaii being notable exemptions. The same can be said for the top ten states for each group: there is no overlap in the top ten list for these groups of women. Women of color officeholders are more likely to be present in southern and western legislatures, and white women officeholders are located in northeastern and midwestern states.

Of course, this could be a function of the minority population within the states. Indeed, the top ten states for women of color very closely correspond to the top ten states with

Table 3.1 State Rankings for Women's Legislative Representation, Pooled Percentages by Group, 1990–2010

Top 10 States for Women's State Legislative Representation

State	Female	Rank	State	White Female	Rank	State	Women of Color	Rank
Washington	35.1%	1	Vermont	32.9%	1	Hawaii	19.2%	1
Vermont	33.1%	2	Washington	32.4%	2	California	9.8%	2
Colorado	33.0%	3	New Hampshire	31.9%	3	New Mexico	9.8%	3
Arizona	32.2%	4	Kansas	27.8%	4	Texas	8.3%	4
New Hampshire	32.2%	5	Nevada	27.6%	5	Maryland	8.2%	5
Nevada	31.4%	6	Colorado	27.6%	6	Arizona	7.6%	6
Kansas	29.8%	7	Minnesota	26.7%	7	Illinois	7.3%	7
Maryland	29.6%	8	Maine	26.5%	8	Georgia	6.7%	8
Connecticut	28.0%	9	Connecticut	25.1%	9	Tennessee	6.1%	9
Minnesota	27.3%	10	Idaho	24.6%	10	Louisiana	5.8%	10

(*Continued*)

Table 3.1 (Continued)

Bottom 10 States for Women's State Legislative Representation

State	Female	Rank	State	White Female	Rank	State	Women of Color	Rank
Tennessee	15.4%	41	Pennsylvania	10.0%	41	West Virginia	0.7%	41
Arkansas	15.0%	42	Tennessee	9.8%	42	Minnesota	0.5%	42
Virginia	14.6%	43	Texas	9.8%	43	Idaho	0.5%	43
Louisiana	12.2%	44	Georgia	9.6%	44	New Hampshire	0.4%	44
Pennsylvania	12.0%	45	Oklahoma	9.4%	45	Wyoming	0.2%	45
Mississippi	11.6%	46	Louisiana	6.9%	46	Vermont	0.2%	46
Oklahoma	11.1%	47	Mississippi	6.7%	47	Maine	0.2%	47
Kentucky	10.7%	48	South Carolina	6.6%	48	South Dakota	0.2%	48
South Carolina	10.0%	49	Hawaii	5.8%	49	Kentucky	0.1%	49
Alabama	8.2%	50	Alabama	3.3%	50	North Dakota	0.1%	50

the highest minority populations.[15] However, both Illinois and Tennessee are ranked in the top ten for women of color legislators, and neither is in the top ten in terms of minority population. Furthermore, two states that rank in the top ten for minority populations, New York and Mississippi, do not rank in the top ten for women of color legislators. This suggests that, although the percentage of the minority population is doing a significant amount of explaining where women of color will serve, it does not explain everything. Hardy-Fanta et al. echoed in the finding "that population numbers alone do not produce descriptive representation. Structural features of state electoral systems, a group's political history, population density, political cohesion and mobilization, among other factors, also weigh into this complex story."[16] I will come back to this point shortly.

Speaking more to the questions at hand, however, what Table 3.1 demonstrates is that patterns of legislative service are not the same for white women and women of color. If we only focus on women as a static category, we miss an interesting part of the story. For example, both Arizona and Maryland rank in the top ten states for the percentage of women legislators. But if the data are broken down by white women and women of color, it is clear that women of color are driving those higher percentages. The reverse can be said regarding female representation for the states that rank the lowest: lower percentages of white women better capture the rankings of the states in the bottom ten. Moreover, four of the states where we see the lowest percentages of white women (Texas, Georgia, Louisiana, and Hawaii) find themselves on the top ten list for legislative service by women of color.

Table 3.2 lists the top ten and bottom ten states for legislators of color, men of color, and women of color by using the pooled average percentage of their representational proportions for the same five points in time.

Legislators of color serve in the highest numbers in western and southern States, with New York being the one northeastern exception. For the bottom ten states, legislators of color are less represented in the Northeast and the Midwest. Again, it appears at first glance that this is most likely a case

Table 3.2 State Rankings for Legislators of Color Representation, Pooled Percentages by Group, 1990–2010

Top 10 States for Legislator of Color's State Representation

State	Legislators of Color	Rank	State	Men of Color	Rank	State	Women of Color	Rank
Hawaii	73.9%	1	Hawaii	55.0%	1	Hawaii	19.2%	1
New Mexico	41.3%	2	New Mexico	33.0%	2	California	9.8%	2
Texas	27.6%	3	Texas	20.2%	3	New Mexico	9.8%	3
California	25.2%	4	Mississippi	18.9%	4	Texas	8.3%	4
Mississippi	23.8%	5	Alabama	17.9%	5	Maryland	8.2%	5
Alabama	22.7%	6	California	17.0%	6	Arizona	7.6%	6
Florida	21.9%	7	Florida	16.4%	7	Illinois	7.3%	7
Maryland	21.1%	8	South Carolina	15.2%	8	Georgia	6.7%	8
Louisiana	20.0%	9	Louisiana	14.2%	9	Tennessee	6.1%	9
New York	19.3%	10	New York	14.0%	10	Louisiana	5.8%	10

Bottom 10 States for Legislator of Color's State Representation

State	Legislators of Color	Rank	State	Men of Color	Rank	State	Women of Color	Rank
Minnesota	2.2%	41	Minnesota	1.7%	41	West Virginia	0.7%	41
South Dakota	2.1%	42	West Virginia	1.3%	42	Minnesota	0.5%	42
West Virginia	2.1%	43	Montana	1.3%	43	Idaho	0.5%	43
Iowa	1.9%	44	Wyoming	1.1%	44	New Hampshire	0.4%	44
Wyoming	1.3%	45	Iowa	0.9%	45	Wyoming	0.2%	45
New Hampshire	1.0%	46	Vermont	0.8%	46	Vermont	0.2%	46
Vermont	1.0%	47	New Hampshire	0.7%	47	Maine	0.2%	47
Idaho	1.0%	48	Maine	0.5%	48	South Dakota	0.2%	48
Maine	0.8%	49	Idaho	0.5%	49	Kentucky	0.1%	49
North Dakota	0.5%	50	North Dakota	0.4%	50	North Dakota	0.1%	50

of the percentage of the minority population in the states. To a certain extent, that may be the case. Two states, however, that are in the top ten in terms of minority population are not ranked in the top ten for legislators of color: Georgia and Arizona. In other words, although minority population may explain quite a large part of the variation in office holding by legislators of color, it does not map perfectly on to the data under investigation. Comparing the top ten states for men of color and women of color, only five states overlap: Hawaii, California, Louisiana, New Mexico, and Texas. This suggests that men of color legislators are driving the high percentages in Alabama, Florida, Mississippi, and New York, whereas women of color are capturing the higher percentages in Maryland. The other top ten states for women of color are not top ten states for legislators of color: Arizona, Georgia, Illinois, and Tennessee.

Does the "top ten" pattern for women of color more closely match the pattern of service by women or by legislators of color? This cut of the data suggests that they more aptly reflect legislators of color—but this reflection is not mirrored perfectly. Similar to the comparison with white female legislators, when we compare men of color to women of color, there are some notable differences. Both gender and race/ethnicity intersect and create a distinct configuration of legislative service by women of color.

WOMEN, WHITE WOMEN, AND WOMEN OF COLOR ACROSS TIME AND STATE

The preceding section provided a broad assessment of where we were more and less likely to see women and legislators of color. This section takes a closer look at the variation across the states and discusses in which states there have been the largest increases and decreases for women, white women, and women of color. Figure 3.1 provides an illustration of the historical pattern of women's state legislative office holding since 1990. From this illustration, it is clear that women, overall, have increased their numbers, white women's descriptive representation has plateaued, and service by women of color has steadily increased.

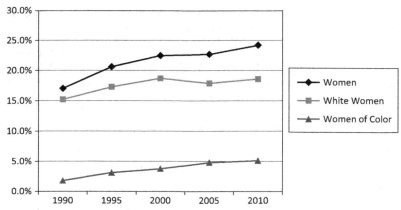

Figure 3.1 Percentage of State Legislative Office Holding for Women, White Women, and Women of Color, 1990–2010

Looking at this trend on a state-by-state basis offers a more detailed picture. Table 3.3 lists the pooled average percentages for women's office holding by state for the same five points in time, as well as the net increase/decrease in office holding, calculated by subtracting the 2010 percentages from the 1990 numbers. The table also reports the comparative categories of white women and women of color legislators. Because the top and bottom ten states were considered earlier, I focus here on the increases and decreases across the states since 1990. What is clear from studying Table 3.3, and as described in the introductory chapter, is that women's growth in office has been uneven across the states. Some states recorded increases in the percentage of women in their legislatures, whereas others experienced decreased in female representation.

On average, women experienced a 7.2% increase in office holding from 1990 to 2010. New Jersey stands as the state with the highest increase in female representation since 1990—17.5% higher than thirty years ago—with New Mexico in second (17.0%), Minnesota taking third place (16.4%), Arkansas ranking fourth (15.6%), and Louisiana coming in at fifth (13.9%). Not all of the news is good. It is discouraging to observe that four states recorded decreases in women office holders—Maine (–2.2%), West Virginia (–3.0%), Wisconsin (–3.8%), and Wyoming (–7.7%). Note that there are

Table 3.3 Pooled Percentage and Increase/Decrease of Women in State Legislatures, by Group and State, 1990–2010

State	Women	Inc/Dec Women	White Women	Inc/Dec White Women	Women of Color	Inc/Dec Women of Color
Alabama	8.2%	7.2%	3.3%	2.1%	4.9%	5.0%
Alaska	20.3%	1.7%	16.3%	0.0%	2.7%	1.7%
Arizona	32.2%	2.2%	24.0%	−7.8%	7.6%	6.7%
Arkansas	15.0%	15.6%	12.1%	14.1%	3.1%	3.0%
California	24.0%	10.9%	14.7%	5.0%	9.8%	8.3%
Colorado	33.0%	9.0%	27.6%	5.0%	4.6%	0.0%
Connecticut	28.0%	10.2%	25.1%	8.0%	2.9%	2.1%
Delaware	24.2%	9.7%	22.3%	6.5%	1.9%	3.2%
Florida	21.6%	7.6%	15.9%	0.0%	5.6%	6.9%
Georgia	17.1%	9.3%	9.6%	1.3%	6.7%	4.2%
Hawaii	25.8%	9.2%	5.8%	−2.6%	19.2%	7.9%
Idaho	26.3%	1.1%	24.6%	−4.0%	0.5%	−0.8%
Illinois	24.5%	9.6%	17.1%	3.4%	7.3%	5.6%
Indiana	18.5%	7.3%	15.7%	5.3%	2.8%	2.0%
Iowa	19.7%	6.6%	18.8%	4.0%	0.9%	2.7%
Kansas	29.8%	4.8%	27.8%	1.8%	2.1%	3.0%
Kentucky	10.7%	10.1%	10.6%	10.1%	0.1%	0.0%
Louisiana	12.2%	13.9%	6.9%	10.4%	5.8%	6.3%
Maine	26.7%	−2.2%	26.5%	−2.2%	0.2%	0.0%
Maryland	29.6%	8.5%	21.4%	−1.1%	8.2%	9.6%
Massachusetts	23.5%	8.5%	21.0%	7.0%	2.5%	1.5%
Michigan	21.4%	10.1%	17.8%	10.8%	3.6%	0.0%
Minnesota	27.3%	16.4%	26.7%	14.9%	0.5%	1.0%
Mississippi	11.6%	8.7%	6.7%	1.7%	4.9%	6.9%
Missouri	20.0%	7.6%	16.4%	3.6%	3.5%	3.6%
Montana	23.5%	8.0%	21.9%	4.7%	1.5%	3.3%
Nebraska	22.9%	0.0%	22.4%	−2.0%	0.8%	4.1%
Nevada	31.4%	9.5%	27.6%	0.0%	2.2%	1.6%
New Hampshire	32.2%	4.7%	31.9%	4.5%	0.4%	0.9%

State	Women	Inc/Dec Women	White Women	Inc/Dec White Women	Women of Color	Inc/Dec Women of Color
New Jersey	16.8%	17.5%	11.3%	6.7%	5.3%	10.0%
New Mexico	24.7%	17.0%	14.8%	4.5%	9.8%	13.4%
New York	19.3%	13.2%	13.8%	11.4%	5.6%	2.4%
North Carolina	19.5%	11.8%	15.6%	4.7%	3.6%	5.9%
North Dakota	16.1%	1.2%	15.6%	-0.6%	0.1%	0.0%
Ohio	19.9%	9.1%	14.8%	5.3%	5.0%	3.8%
Oklahoma	11.1%	2.7%	9.4%	2.7%	1.9%	0.7%
Oregon	27.1%	8.9%	23.6%	8.9%	3.6%	0.0%
Pennsylvania	12.0%	8.7%	10.0%	6.3%	1.9%	1.6%
Rhode Island	20.6%	6.8%	17.0%	0.0%	2.7%	2.0%
South Carolina	10.0%	1.2%	6.6%	0.0%	3.5%	1.8%
South Dakota	17.5%	1.0%	17.3%	1.0%	0.2%	0.0%
Tennessee	15.4%	9.1%	9.8%	4.5%	6.1%	6.8%
Texas	18.0%	13.3%	9.8%	6.6%	8.3%	7.2%
Utah	17.9%	10.6%	16.9%	7.7%	0.8%	1.9%
Vermont	33.1%	3.9%	32.9%	3.9%	0.2%	0.0%
Virginia	14.6%	8.6%	10.4%	4.3%	4.3%	5.0%
Washington	35.1%	3.4%	32.4%	2.0%	3.1%	3.4%
West Virginia	16.9%	-3.0%	16.1%	-4.5%	0.7%	1.5%
Wisconsin	24.2%	-3.8%	21.7%	-4.5%	2.6%	0.8%
Wyoming	19.1%	-7.7%	18.4%	-7.8%	0.2%	-1.1%
Average	21.4%	7.2%	17.5%	3.4%	3.7%	3.3%

significant differences in the region of both the increasing and decreasing states, meaning that this decrease is not necessarily a "regional" effect. The remainder of the states registers stagnant or weak increases in female representation.

If we disaggregate by race/ethnicity, an interesting picture emerges. The previously noted increases and decreases in legislative service for all women are quite different if we investigate white women and women of color separately. First, on average, white female legislators increased their percentages by 3.4% compared to their 1990 numbers, and women of color legislators came in slightly lower at 3.3%. In terms of high states, white women legislators increased their descriptive representation the most in Minnesota (14.9%), Arkansas (14.1%), New York (11.4%), Michigan (10.8%), and Louisiana (10.4%). Women of color recorded the highest gains in New Mexico (13.4%), Maryland (9.6%), California (8.3%), Hawaii (7.9%), and Texas (7.2%).

White women witnessed a decrease in their representational levels since 1990 in 10 states, a full 20% of the legislatures across the United States! In Arizona (–7.8%), Hawaii (–2.6%), Idaho (–4.0%), Maine (–2.2%), Maryland (–1.1%), Nebraska (–2.0%), North Dakota (–0.6%), West Virginia (–4.5%), Wisconsin (–4.5%), and Wyoming (–1.1%), white female legislators lost representation at the state level since 1990. Women of color, however, saw a decrease in their numbers in only *two* states—Idaho (–0.8%) and Wyoming (–1.1%). In fact, women of color increased their numbers in all of the states that registered a decrease in white female representation except for Idaho and Wyoming, where they also showed decreases, and North Dakota, which remained constant. In other words, where white women lost representation, the increase in women of color legislators made up for some of those losses.

This means that, on average, women of color have steadily increased their numbers in state legislatures whereas white women have steadily decreased in numbers. To say it another way, the percentage increases that we see in women state legislators is primarily women of color and not white women. For example, more than three-fourths of the 17% increase in women legislators that New Mexico experienced from 1990 to 2010 was due to women of color. New Jersey witnessed a similar phenomenon, with more than half of their increase in female representation comprising women of color. In places such as Minnesota and Arkansas, where white women's gains were highest, women of color increased their numbers as well.

To summarize, women in the aggregate experienced an increase in state legislative office holding from 1990 to

Mapping the Terrain 79

2010. However, this growth in numbers was not even across state or among racial/ethnic groups. There are distinct differences in the pattern of the descriptive representation of white female and women of color legislators, especially in how this representation has increased or decreased since 1990. The next step is to see if women of color mirror the trends in office holding compared to their men of color counterparts.

LEGISLATORS OF COLOR, MEN OF COLOR, AND WOMEN OF COLOR ACROSS TIME AND STATE

Like the percentage of women legislators, the proportion of legislators of color has also seen an increase over time, especially after the redistricting efforts of 1990. This section describes the differences we see in legislators of color, men of color, and women of color office holding across the fifty states. Similar to the preceding one, Figure 3.2 graphs the historical pattern of state office holding by legislators of color since 1990 broken down by gender. From this diagram, it is evident that legislators of color, overall, have increased their numbers, whereas the legislative numbers for men of color have plateaued, and, as demonstrated in Figure 3.1, service by women of color has steadily increased.

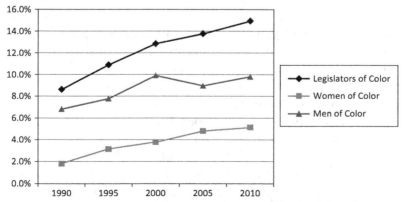

Figure 3.2 Percentage of State Legislative Office Holding for Legislators of Color, Men of Color, and Women of Color, 1990–2010

Turning to a state-by-state analysis of this trend, Table 3.4 lists the pooled average percentages for office holding by legislators of color by state for the same five points in time, the net increase/decrease in office holding since 1990, and the comparative categories of men of color and women of color legislators. Again, because I provided a thorough treatment of the top and bottom ten states earlier, my primary interest in the following is to examine the increases and decreases across the states since 1990.

Similar to their female counterparts, legislators of color experienced an increase in their representational numbers on average, up 6.3% from 1990. The highest gains were recorded in California (20.8%), New Mexico (17.0%), Mississippi (16.1%), Oklahoma (16.1%), and Hawaii (14.5%). One of these states, New Mexico, is where there were also large increases in female representation generally, but women of color specifically. Three states registered decreases: Colorado (–6.6%), Oregon (–1.1%), and Vermont (–0.6%). There is less regional variation than documented for women overall, with most of the increases in descriptive representation by legislators of color taking place mainly in the western and southern states.

If we compare men of color legislators to women of color legislators, there are again some intriguing differences. Men of color increased their percentages on average by 8.6%, with the highest increases since 1990 in Oklahoma (15.4%), California (12.5%), Alaska (11.7%), Nevada (11.1%), and Michigan (9.5%). Of the states that recorded the highest increases for both genders, only California is shared by both men and women of color legislators. Curiously similar to white female legislators, men of color legislators lost representation in *ten* states: Arizona (–2.2%), Colorado (–6.0%), Kansas (–1.2%), Missouri (–1.5%), Nebraska (–2.0%), Ohio (–0.8%), Oregon (–1.1%), Rhode Island (–2.0%), Tennessee (–2.3%), and Vermont (–0.6%).

This adds weight to the argument that the increases since 1990 in office holding by legislators of color overall are primarily due to women of color. Women of color recorded increases in all of the states where men of color recorded decreases, with the exceptions of Colorado, Oregon, and

Table 3.4 Pooled Percentage and Increase/Decrease of Legislators of Color in State Legislatures by Group and State, 1990–2010

State	Legislators of Color	Inc/Dec Legislators of Color	Men of Color	Inc/Dec Men of Color	Women of Color	Inc/Dec Women of Color
Alabama	22.7%	8.6%	17.9%	3.6%	4.9%	5.0%
Alaska	12.7%	13.3%	10.0%	11.7%	2.7%	1.7%
Arizona	19.1%	4.4%	12.2%	-2.2%	7.6%	6.7%
Arkansas	9.6%	5.9%	6.5%	3.0%	3.1%	3.0%
California	25.2%	20.8%	17.0%	12.5%	9.8%	8.3%
Colorado	12.4%	-6.0%	8.4%	-6.0%	4.6%	0.0%
Connecticut	10.2%	7.5%	7.6%	5.3%	2.9%	2.1%
Delaware	7.1%	4.8%	5.2%	1.6%	1.9%	3.2%
Florida	21.9%	12.5%	16.4%	5.6%	5.6%	6.9%
Georgia	19.2%	12.3%	12.5%	8.1%	6.7%	4.2%
Hawaii	73.9%	14.5%	55.0%	6.6%	19.2%	7.9%
Idaho	1.0%	0.0%	0.5%	0.8%	0.5%	-0.8%
Illinois	18.3%	9.6%	11.1%	4.0%	7.3%	5.6%
Indiana	8.1%	2.7%	5.3%	0.7%	2.8%	2.0%
Iowa	1.9%	4.0%	0.9%	1.3%	0.9%	2.7%
Kansas	5.8%	1.8%	3.8%	-1.2%	2.1%	3.0%

(*Continued*)

Table 3.4 (Continued)

State	Legislators of Color	Inc/Dec Legislators of Color	Men of Color	Inc/Dec Men of Color	Women of Color	Inc/Dec Women of Color
Kentucky	3.6%	4.3%	3.5%	4.3%	0.1%	0.0%
Louisiana	20.0%	6.3%	14.2%	0.0%	5.8%	6.3%
Maine	0.8%	1.1%	0.5%	1.1%	0.2%	0.0%
Maryland	21.1%	11.7%	12.9%	2.1%	8.2%	9.6%
Massachusetts	4.6%	1.5%	2.2%	0.0%	2.5%	1.5%
Michigan	14.6%	9.5%	11.1%	9.5%	3.6%	0.0%
Minnesota	2.2%	3.5%	1.7%	2.5%	0.5%	1.0%
Mississippi	23.8%	16.1%	18.9%	9.2%	4.9%	6.9%
Missouri	8.9%	2.0%	5.5%	-1.5%	3.5%	3.6%
Montana	2.8%	6.7%	1.3%	3.3%	1.5%	3.3%
Nebraska	3.3%	2.0%	2.4%	-2.0%	0.8%	4.1%
Nevada	12.4%	12.7%	10.5%	11.1%	2.2%	1.6%
New Hampshire	1.0%	1.2%	0.7%	0.2%	0.4%	0.9%
New Jersey	14.8%	11.7%	9.8%	1.7%	5.3%	10.0%
New Mexico	41.3%	17.0%	33.0%	3.6%	9.8%	13.4%
New York	19.3%	10.9%	14.0%	8.5%	5.6%	2.4%
North Carolina	15.1%	8.8%	11.4%	2.9%	3.6%	5.9%

North Dakota	0.5%	1.3%	0.4%	1.3%	0.1%	0.0%
Ohio	12.3%	3.0%	7.3%	-0.8%	5.0%	3.8%
Oklahoma	7.7%	16.1%	5.8%	15.4%	1.9%	0.7%
Oregon	5.6%	-1.1%	2.2%	-1.1%	3.6%	0.0%
Pennsylvania	8.1%	3.2%	6.2%	1.6%	1.9%	1.6%
Rhode Island	5.5%	0.0%	3.1%	-2.0%	2.7%	2.0%
South Carolina	18.7%	10.6%	15.2%	8.8%	3.5%	1.8%
South Dakota	2.1%	2.9%	1.9%	2.9%	0.2%	0.0%
Tennessee	12.7%	4.5%	6.7%	-2.3%	6.1%	6.8%
Texas	27.6%	7.7%	20.2%	0.6%	8.3%	7.2%
Utah	2.9%	4.8%	2.3%	2.9%	0.8%	1.9%
Vermont	1.0%	-0.6%	0.8%	-0.6%	0.2%	0.0%
Virginia	10.6%	6.4%	6.3%	1.4%	4.3%	5.0%
Washington	6.9%	6.8%	4.2%	3.4%	3.1%	3.4%
West Virginia	2.1%	1.5%	1.3%	0.0%	0.7%	1.5%
Wisconsin	6.1%	3.0%	3.5%	2.3%	2.6%	0.8%
Wyoming	1.3%	2.2%	1.1%	3.3%	0.2%	-1.1%
Average	12.2%	6.3%	8.6%	3.0%	3.7%	3.3%

Vermont, where the numbers for women of color remained fixed. New Mexico stands out once more: the increased numbers in legislators of color are due to women of color.[17]

Just by looking at the descriptive data, it is apparent that women of color are increasing their numbers in states where men of color legislators are not. What is more is that women of color are not increasing their numbers in states where white women are either. Instead, they seem to be heightening their numbers in states that do not overlap with either of their gender or their racial/ethnic counterparts. In other words, race and gender are intersecting for women of color and creating an entirely different representational pattern that cannot be pieced out based on gender or race alone.

WOMEN OF COLOR AND THE GENDER GAP IN OFFICE HOLDING

Up to this point, I have focused on the geographical variation in office holding for women legislators and legislators of color—measured as the percentage of their presence within the total legislative body—and attempted to tease out the differences in the descriptive representational patterns among white women, women of color, and men of color. Identifying how the geographical variation in office holding by women of color only takes us so far. Although it is important to understanding that the pattern of legislative service by women of color is unique across the fifty states compared to white female legislators, it is equally essential to determine where and why they are serving at proportionally higher rates than are their white female counterparts. This section takes up that second research question of interest in this book: the smaller gender gap in office holding for legislators of color compared to white legislators.

The gender gap is measured as the difference between the male and female percentages in the legislature, using the pooled average for each state for the same five points in time, with negative numbers indicating that women serve at higher rates than men. For instance, in Alabama, based on the pooled average, men composed 91.8% of the state

Mapping the Terrain 85

legislature, whereas women held 8.2% of the seats. Therefore, the average gender gap across the twenty-year time span under investigation in Alabama was 83.7%. Of interest here is the white gender gap versus the legislator of color gender gap. The white gender gap is the difference between the pooled average percentage of white males and white females in the legislature, and the legislator of color gender gap is the difference between the pooled average percentage of men of color and women of color in the state legislative body.

This section proceeds by first briefly addressing the state-by-state variation in these same gaps and then presenting a ranked order of the top and bottom ten states for both the white gender gap and the legislator of color gender gap, as well as the ranked order of states where there were the largest and smallest increases in these same gaps.

Table 3.5 lists the pooled average percentages for the gender gap in general, the white gender gap, and the legislator of color gender gap, as well as the increases and decreases in these gaps since 1990 for all fifty states.[18]

On average, the gender gap across the states was 57.3%, decreasing by 13.9% since 1990. The white gender gap averaged 59.9% and decreased by 11.9% from the 1990 baseline. The legislator of color gender gap averaged 4.9% and decreased by 0.9% since 1990. Which states have the highest and lowest gender gaps? Is this the same for whites and legislators of color? Table 3.6 presents the state rankings, both the highest and lowest, for the gender gap overall, the white gender gap, and the legislator of color gender gap. Overall, there are no surprises in terms of the states with the highest and lowest gender gap in general. They are the all southern states, with the exception of Pennsylvania (76.0%). Alabama ranks first with an 83.7% gap. The states with the lowest gaps are mainly northeastern and western states, with the exceptions of Maryland (40.9%) and Kansas (40.4%).

Looking at the white and legislator of color gap separately, are there any similarities between the white and legislator of color gender gaps? Four states rank in the top ten of states with the highest gender gaps on both lists: Alabama, South Carolina, Louisiana, and Mississippi. Two states are common in the rankings of states with the lowest

Table 3.5 Pooled Percentage and Increase/Decrease in the Gender Gap in State Legislatures by Group and State, 1990–2010

State	Gender Gap	% Inc/Dec in Gender Gap	White Gender Gap	Inc/Dec White Gender Gap	Legislator of Color Gender Gap	Inc/Dec Legislator of Color Gender Gap
Alabama	83.7%	−14.3%	91.5%	−6.6%	13.0%	−1.4%
Alaska	59.3%	−3.3%	62.2%	−6.4%	7.3%	10.0%
Arizona	35.6%	−4.4%	39.0%	7.7%	4.7%	−8.9%
Arkansas	70.1%	−31.1%	73.6%	−29.0%	3.4%	0.0%
California	52.0%	−21.7%	61.1%	−15.6%	7.2%	4.2%
Colorado	34.0%	−18.0%	35.2%	−15.9%	3.8%	−6.0%
Connecticut	44.0%	−20.3%	43.9%	−22.2%	4.7%	3.2%
Delaware	51.6%	−19.4%	51.9%	−16.1%	3.2%	−1.6%
Florida	56.8%	−15.0%	58.9%	−7.6%	10.8%	−1.3%
Georgia	65.8%	−18.6%	74.1%	−16.3%	5.8%	3.8%
Hawaii	48.4%	−18.4%	44.9%	−63.6%	35.8%	−1.3%
Idaho	49.2%	6.3%	49.7%	4.8%	0.0%	1.6%
Illinois	51.0%	−19.2%	57.8%	−14.2%	3.7%	−1.7%
Indiana	62.9%	−14.7%	65.7%	−12.4%	2.5%	−1.3%
Iowa	60.5%	−13.3%	61.6%	−9.8%	0.0%	−1.3%

Kansas	40.4%	-9.7%	41.0%	-4.9%	1.7%	-4.2%
Kentucky	78.6%	-20.3%	77.9%	-22.1%	3.3%	4.3%
Louisiana	75.6%	-27.8%	83.7%	-19.1%	8.3%	-6.3%
Maine	46.7%	4.3%	46.7%	3.7%	0.5%	0.5%
Maryland	40.9%	-17.0%	45.6%	-4.2%	4.7%	-7.4%
Massachusetts	53.0%	-17.0%	55.9%	-15.3%	-0.3%	-1.5%
Michigan	57.3%	-20.3%	58.3%	-28.5%	7.4%	9.5%
Minnesota	45.5%	-32.8%	45.1%	-33.5%	1.2%	1.5%
Mississippi	76.8%	-17.2%	82.3%	-7.5%	13.9%	2.3%
Missouri	60.0%	-15.2%	63.7%	-9.7%	2.0%	-5.1%
Montana	53.0%	-16.0%	54.8%	-12.6%	-0.2%	-1.3%
Nebraska	54.3%	0.0%	54.4%	7.6%	1.6%	-6.1%
Nevada	37.1%	-19.0%	33.0%	-27.1%	8.3%	9.5%
New Hampshire	35.7%	-9.4%	35.7%	-8.4%	0.3%	-0.7%
New Jersey	66.3%	-35.0%	72.7%	-21.4%	4.5%	-8.3%

(Continued)

Table 3.5 (Continued)

State	Gender Gap	% Inc/Dec in Gender Gap	White Gender Gap	Inc/Dec White Gender Gap	Legislator of Color Gender Gap	Inc/Dec Legislator of Color Gender Gap
New Mexico	50.7%	−33.9%	48.8%	−25.7%	23.2%	−9.8%
New York	61.4%	−26.5%	65.5%	−30.8%	8.4%	6.2%
North Carolina	60.9%	−23.5%	62.4%	−17.8%	7.8%	−2.9%
North Dakota	68.6%	1.3%	68.7%	0.9%	0.4%	0.6%
Ohio	60.3%	−18.2%	66.1%	−13.0%	2.3%	−4.5%
Oklahoma	77.7%	−5.4%	79.9%	−7.8%	3.9%	14.8%
Oregon	45.8%	−17.8%	50.1%	−18.0%	−1.3%	−1.1%
Pennsylvania	76.0%	−17.4%	77.9%	−16.4%	4.3%	0.0%
Rhode Island	61.0%	−2.7%	64.2%	1.4%	0.4%	−4.0%
South Carolina	80.0%	−2.4%	84.1%	−0.7%	11.6%	7.1%
South Dakota	65.0%	−1.9%	64.6%	−3.1%	2.1%	1.9%
Tennessee	69.1%	−18.2%	78.4%	−6.3%	0.6%	−9.1%
Texas	64.0%	−26.5%	72.9%	−19.2%	11.9%	−6.6%
Utah	64.2%	−21.2%	64.6%	−19.3%	1.9%	0.0%
Vermont	33.8%	−7.8%	33.6%	−7.5%	0.6%	−0.6%

Virginia	70.9%	-17.1%	76.9%	-9.6%	2.0%	-3.6%
Washington	29.8%	-6.8%	31.3%	-4.6%	1.1%	0.0%
West Virginia	66.3%	6.0%	67.1%	8.6%	0.6%	-1.5%
Wisconsin	51.5%	7.6%	53.9%	8.2%	0.9%	1.5%
Wyoming	61.8%	15.6%	62.1%	12.7%	1.1%	4.4%
Average	57.3%	-13.9%	59.9%	-11.9%	4.9%	-0.9%

Table 3.6 State Rankings for Gender Gap, Pooled Percentages by Group, 1990–2010

States with the Highest Gender Gaps

State	Gender Gap	Rank	State	White Gender Gap	Rank	State	Legislator of Color Gender Gap	Rank
Alabama	83.7%	1	Alabama	91.5%	1	Hawaii	35.8%	1
South Carolina	80.0%	2	South Carolina	84.1%	2	New Mexico	23.2%	2
Kentucky	78.6%	3	Louisiana	83.7%	3	Mississippi	13.9%	3
Oklahoma	77.7%	4	Mississippi	82.3%	4	Alabama	13.0%	4
Mississippi	76.8%	5	Oklahoma	79.9%	5	Texas	11.9%	5
Pennsylvania	76.0%	6	Tennessee	78.4%	6	South Carolina	11.6%	6
Louisiana	75.6%	7	Pennsylvania	77.9%	7	Florida	10.8%	7
Virginia	70.9%	8	Kentucky	77.9%	8	New York	8.4%	8
Arkansas	70.1%	9	Virginia	76.9%	9	Louisiana	8.3%	9
Tennessee	69.1%	10	Georgia	74.1%	10	Nevada	8.3%	10

States with the Lowest Gender Gaps

State	Gender Gap	Rank	State	White Gender Gap	Rank	State	Legislator of Color Gender Gap	Rank
Washington	29.8%	1	Washington	31.3%	1	Oregon	-1.3%	1
Vermont	33.8%	2	Nevada	33.0%	2	Massachusetts	-0.3%	2
Colorado	34.0%	3	Vermont	33.6%	3	Montana	-0.2%	3
Arizona	35.6%	4	Colorado	35.2%	4	Iowa	0.0%	4
New Hampshire	35.7%	5	New Hampshire	35.7%	5	Idaho	0.0%	5
Nevada	37.1%	6	Arizona	39.0%	6	New Hampshire	0.3%	6
Kansas	40.4%	7	Kansas	41.0%	7	North Dakota	0.4%	7
Maryland	40.9%	8	Connecticut	43.9%	8	Rhode Island	0.4%	8
Connecticut	44.0%	9	Hawaii	44.9%	9	Maine	0.5%	9
Minnesota	45.5%	10	Minnesota	45.1%	10	Vermont	0.6%	10

gaps: Vermont and New Hampshire. That being said, it becomes clear that the states with the highest white gender gap more closely resemble the overall gender gap. The only state that does not match up is Georgia (74.1%). White women continue to do poorly in southern states, with the exception, again, of Pennsylvania (77.9%).[19] States with the lowest white gender gap also mirror the overall gender gap, with the exception of Hawaii (44.9%).

For the states with the highest legislator of color gender gap, the results are counter-intuitive based on what has been presented so far. In the last section, I showed that the top ten states for women of color legislators, and the ones where they were seeing the highest increases in office holding, were mainly western and southern states. Table 3.6 documents, however, that these are also the states still with higher-than-average legislator of color gender gaps. For instance, Hawaii registered the highest percentages of women of color legislators, but it is also the state with the highest legislator of color gender gap (35.8%). New Mexico was the state where women of color had made the largest gains since 1990, increasing their numbers by 13.4%. Yet, New Mexico has the second-highest legislator of color gender gap, at 23.2%. So, although women of color have clearly made great strides over the last thirty years, especially in western and southern states, these are also the same states with the largest gap in their office holding. Gender is still a relevant indicator of legislative service.

States with the lowest legislator of color gender gap are primarily northeastern and midwestern states, with Montana, Massachusetts, and Oregon actually registering negative numbers, meaning that are more women of color legislators in those states than men of color. Of course, it can be said that this is a function of number—there are very, very few legislators of color in those states, male or female. As such, being one of two legislators of color is not exactly a coup.

One might say, however, that as the minority population increases in a state, the likelihood that a legislator of color is a woman decreases. The reverse seems to be true for white women: the higher the minority population, the more likely it is that a white legislator will be a woman. Take Hawaii, for example. It is a bottom ten gender gap state for women of color, but a top ten gender gap state for white women. We see the same pattern regarding Nevada, where the white women seem to be doing better, but women of color are not. To be sure, women of color still register much smaller gaps in office holding, even in these states. In Nevada, the white gender gap is 33.0% and the legislator of color gender gap is only 8.3%. Nevertheless, the point is that both race/ethnicity and gender are intersecting in terms of state legislative service.

Where have there been the largest increases and decreases in the gender gap? Table 3.7 list a rank order of the states with the highest increases and highest decreases in the gender gap, the white gender gap, and the legislator of color gender gap.

The gender gap in office holding overall has increased the most in Wyoming (15.6%) and has decreased the most in New Jersey (−35.0%). Interestingly, there does not appear to be a true regional pattern in these increases and decreases. The same can be said when comparing the white and legislator of color increases and decreases: states ranking highest and lowest on both lists do not follow a clear regional arrangement. Both the white and the legislator of color gender gap increased in South Carolina and Wyoming and decreased in New Mexico and New Jersey. Those are the only overlaps between white women and women of color in terms of the top and bottom states. One might say that Wyoming and South Carolina were both unfavorable states for women over the twenty-year time span under consideration, because both the white and legislator of color gender gaps ranked on the top ten states with increasing gaps, whereas New Mexico and New Jersey provided more favorable environments, with both of those states ranking among the top ten states to register decreases.

The white gender gap decreased the most in Hawaii (−63.6%), and women of color did the best in New Mexico, with a 9.8% decrease in the gender gap there since 1990. Other states show mixed results when comparing the white and legislator of color gender gap: Arizona closed the legislator of color gap by 8.9% but increased the white gender gap by 7.7% The same can be said for Nebraska, where the

Table 3.7 State Rankings for Increase/Decrease in Gender Gaps, Pooled Percentages by Group, 1990–2010

States with the Highest Increases in Gender Gap

State	Gender Gap	Rank	State	White Gender Gap	Rank	State	Legislator of Color Gender Gap	Rank
Wyoming	15.6%	1	Wyoming	12.7%	1	Oklahoma	14.8%	1
Wisconsin	7.6%	2	West Virginia	8.6%	2	Alaska	10.0%	2
Idaho	6.3%	3	Wisconsin	8.2%	3	Nevada	9.5%	3
West Virginia	6.0%	4	Arizona	7.7%	4	Michigan	9.5%	4
Maine	4.3%	5	Nebraska	7.6%	5	South Carolina	7.1%	5
North Dakota	1.3%	6	Idaho	4.8%	6	New York	6.2%	6
Nebraska	0.0%	7	Maine	3.7%	7	Wyoming	4.4%	7
South Dakota	-1.9%	8	Rhode Island	1.4%	8	Kentucky	4.3%	8
South Carolina	-2.4%	9	North Dakota	0.9%	9	California	4.2%	9
Rhode Island	-2.7%	10	South Carolina	-0.7%	10	Georgia	3.8%	10

States with the Highest Decreases in the Gender Gap

State	Gender Gap	Rank	State	White Gender Gap	Rank	State	Legislator of Color Gender Gap	Rank
New Jersey	−35.0%	1	Hawaii	−63.6%	1	New Mexico	−9.8%	1
New Mexico	−33.9%	2	Minnesota	−33.5%	2	Tennessee	−9.1%	2
Minnesota	−32.8%	3	New York	−30.8%	3	Arizona	−8.9%	3
Arkansas	−31.1%	4	Arkansas	−29.0%	4	New Jersey	−8.3%	4
Louisiana	−27.8%	5	Michigan	−28.5%	5	Maryland	−7.4%	5
New York	−26.5%	6	Nevada	−27.1%	6	Texas	−6.6%	6
Texas	−26.5%	7	New Mexico	−25.7%	7	Louisiana	−6.3%	7
North Carolina	−23.5%	8	Connecticut	−22.2%	8	Nebraska	−6.1%	8
California	−21.7%	9	Kentucky	−22.1%	9	Colorado	−6.0%	9
Utah	−21.2%	10	New Jersey	−21.4%	10	Missouri	−5.1%	10

legislator of color gap decreased by 6.1% and the white gap increased by 7.6%. However, white women closed the gap in Michigan by 28.5%, and women of color experienced a widening of the gap by 9.5%. Kentucky registered a 22.1% decrease in the white gender gap and a 4.3% increase in the legislator of color gender gap. Race/ethnicity, then, appears to be particularly relevant for women in Arizona, Nebraska, Michigan, and Kentucky. Indeed, Arizona ranked within the top ten states for female representation overall (see Table 3.1), so one might conclude that this is at least in part to women of color increasing their numbers within that state. However, the decrease in the white gender gap in Kentucky did not do enough to pull it out of the bottom ten states for female representation overall (Table 3.1).

CONCLUSION

Up to this point, we have taken a descriptive historical look at the percentage increases and decreases in women and minority office holders. The main points that should be taken away from this analysis are that women of color legislators do not perfectly match either of their gender or their racial counterparts. Their service pattern differs in both percentages and variation across the states in comparison to white women and men of color.

Looking closely at all of the rankings presented in this chapter, what do the top ten and bottom ten states have in common? Two things stand out: region and minority population distribution, both of which overlap. The percentage of the minority population is obviously driving most of these results for legislators of color, but it is not pushing *all* of the outcomes. As noted earlier, the legislator of color gender gap present puzzling results. The same states that have the highest percentages of women of color legislators, often cited as a result of the minority population within the state, also have the *highest* legislator of color gender gaps. If gender was not intersecting with race/ethnicity, *there would be no gender gap among legislators of color*. Gender, for women of color, matters—perhaps not as much as it does for white female legislators, who register much

Mapping the Terrain 97

higher gaps in office holding—especially in states with higher minority populations. What else is at play here? The next two chapters investigate this puzzle deeper through correlation and regression tests to see if these initial patterns are confirmed.

NOTES

1. Center for American Women and Politics, "Women of Color in State Legislatures 1990, 1995, 2000, 2005, and 2010" (New Brunswick, New Jersey: Eagleton Institute for Politics, Rutgers, State University of New Jersey, November 2010), personal request.
2. Center for American Women and Politics, "Women in State Legislatures 2010" (New Brunswick, NJ: Eagleton Institute for Politics, Rutgers, State University of New Jersey, 2010), http://www.cawp.rutgers.edu/fast_facts/levels_of_office/documents/stleg.pdf.
3. Barbara Norrander and Clyde Wilcox, "The Geography of Gender Power: Women in State Legislatures," in *Women and Elective Office: Past, Present, and Future*, ed. by Sue Thomas and Clyde Wilcox (New York: Oxford University Press, 1998): 103–117.
4. Center for American Women and Politics, "Women of Color in Elective Office 2010" (New Brunswick, NJ: Eagleton Institute for Politics, Rutgers, State University of New Jersey, 2010), http://www.cawp.rutgers.edu/fast_facts/levels_of_office/documents/color.pdf.
5. Data for the five points in time was collected from the Center for American Women and Politics (CAWP), the Joint Center, the National Association for Latino Elected Officials (NALEO), the National Asian Pacific American Political Almanac, and the National Conference of State Legislatures. For a description of this process, see the section in this chapter titled "A Note on the Data."
6. Chapters 4 and 5 discuss this finding in more detail. In short, however, although the percentage of the minority population is a significant predictor of where women of color serve, other indicators are also useful for explaining their geographical variation as well as the smaller gender gap in office holding among legislators of color.
7. UCLA Asian American Studies Center and the Asian Pacific American Institute for Congressional Studies. *National Asian Pacific American Political Almanac*. Los Angeles, CA: UCLA Asian American Studies Center Press.

8. Pei-te Lien, Carol Hardy-Fanta, Dianne M. Pinderhughes, and Christine Marie Sierra, "Expanding Categorization at the Intersection of Race and Gender: 'Women of Color' as a Political Category for African American, Latina, Asian American, and American Indian Women" (paper delivered at the Annual Meeting of the American Political Science Association, Boston, August 27–31, 2008).
9. Geron and Lai also find similarities between Latino and Asian American elected officials. See Kim Geron and James S. Lai, "Beyond Symbolic Representation: A Comparison of the Electoral Pathways and Policy Priorities of Asian American and Latino Elected Officials," *Asian Law Journal* 9 (May 2002): 41–81.
10. Carol Hardy-Fanta, Pei-te Lien, Christine Marie Sierra, and Dianne M. Pinderhughes, "A New Look at Paths to Political Office: Moving Women of Color from the Margins to the Center" (paper delivered at the American Political Science Association's annual meeting, Chicago, August 30-September 2, 2007), 29.
11. Mary Hawkesworth, "Congressional Enactments of Race-Gender: Toward a Theory of Raced-Gendered Institutions," *American Political Science Review* 97, no. 4 (November 2003): 529–550.
12. Ibid., 532.
13. Bernard Grofman and Lisa Handley, "Minority Population Proportion and Black and Hispanic Congressional Success in the 1970s and 1980s," *American Politics Quarterly* 17, no. 4 (October 1989): 437.
14. Katharine Q. Seelye, "From Congress to Halls of State, in New Hampshire, Women Rule," *New York Times*, January 2, 2013, A1.
15. The ten states with the highest percentages of minority population, pooled and averaged for the years under investigation (1990–2010), and ranked from highest to lowest, are Hawaii, New Mexico, California, Texas, Mississippi, Maryland, Louisiana, Georgia, New York, and Arizona.
16. Carol Hardy-Fanta, Pei-te Lien, Dianne M. Pinderhughes, and Christine Marie Sierra, "Gender, Race, and Descriptive Representation in the United States: Findings from the Gender and Multicultural Leadership Project," *Journal of Women, Politics and Policy* 28, no. 3–4 (2006): 22.
17. Fraga et al. confirms this trend as well, with those authors noting that New Mexico had the greatest percentage increase in Latina representation, but Latino representation remained constant. California, however, demonstrated the same growth rate in representation for both Latinos and Latinas and gender. See Luis Ricardo Fraga, Linda Lopez, Valeria Martinez-Ebers,

and Ricardo Ramirez, "Gender and Ethnicity: Patterns of Electoral Success and Legislative Advocacy among Latina and Latino State Officials in Four States," *Journal of Women, Politics and Policy* 28, no. 3–4 (2006): 122–145.
18. The increase/decrease in the gender gaps is measured by subtracting the 2010 gender gap from the 1990 gender gap, with negative numbers representing a decrease. Because there were either no men or women of color in a few states for certain years, the percentages for Maine, Montana, and North Dakota are based on the increase/decrease from 2000 to 2010, and the percentages for Texas and Utah are based on the increase/decrease from 1995 to 2010.
19. Pennsylvania has consistently found itself ranked in the bottom ten states for women's legislative representation. This northeastern state stands out among the sea of southern states that typically compose that lamentable distinction.

4 Geographical Variation at the Intersection

The last chapter established that the variation in the descriptive pattern for women of color's office holding is unique when compared to both their gender and racial counterparts. I documented that women of color and white women were most likely to be present in different states, and that the same could be said if women of color's legislative presence was compared to men of color as well. What explains women of color's distinctive geographical variation in office holding across the fifty states?

This chapter begins to look at one of the primary research questions in this book, namely, the variation in office holding across the states and how this differs at the intersection of gender and race/ethnicity. What is it about a state's particular contextual and structural environment that makes it more or less conducive to women's office holding? And, how does race/ethnicity intersect with gender within these same environments? If all state environments were equally women-friendly, then there would not be a variation in women's office holding across the states. If all states were equally race/ethnic-friendly, then there would not be a variation in legislator of color's office holding across the states. And, if the intersection of gender and race/ethnicity did not matter, then we would see women of color equally distributed across the states among both women and legislators of color. None of these statements is supported by the descriptive data presented in the last chapter. Gender, race/ethnicity, and the intersection of both, matter at the state level.

As discussed in Chapter 3, two discernible patterns may account for the variation in office holding by women of color: region and minority population distribution. However, I also noted that, while important, minority population does not seem to be the only factor driving the variation. If it was only minority population, then there would be higher percentages of women of color in, say, New York and Mississippi. Indeed, these states experience high rates of legislator of color office holding, but men of color are mostly responsible for these numbers, a topic that is more fully taken up in Chapter 5 when the differential gender gaps are explored.

Furthermore, the same logic cannot be applied to the geographical variation in women's office holding—women's percentage of the population does not vary across states but their descriptive representational percentages do. In Chapter 2, I reviewed the women and politics literature that has attempted to explain the variation in women's state legislative service, as well as the relevant studies within the race and ethnic politics literature on the same topic. The set of hypotheses listed Chapter 2 closely followed the findings from both of those areas of research and will be tested here. My aim is to assess whether or not the conventional wisdom applies equally to both white women and women of color legislators. Does the model more accurately predict the variation in legislative service by white women and women of color?

TESTING THE VARIATION MODEL AT THE INTERSECTIONS: DATA AND METHODOLOGY

The question guiding this chapter pertains to the geographical variation in women legislators across the states and how this varies by the race/ethnicity. In other words, given that a legislator is a woman, what has an impact on the chances that she is a white woman or a woman of color? For comparative purposes, I also look at the geographical variation in office holding by legislators of color across the states and at how this varies by gender. Previous work on the topic suggests that a set of variables perform fairly well in explaining this variation. My goal is to test the effectiveness of these factors from an intersectional perspective by placing women of color at the center of analysis. Accordingly, I collected data that included the percentage of women and men serving in all fifty state legislatures, disaggregated by race/ethnicity, as well as several state-level demographic and legislative indicators for a twenty-year time span (1990–2010).[1] As fully discussed in Chapter 3, five dependent variables were constructed: the percentage of women in the state legislature, the percentage of white women, the percentage of legislators of color, the percentage of women of color, and the percentage of men of color (African American, Latina, Asian American, and American Indian). All five dependent variables were first calculated as the percentage of the total legislature for each of the fifty states for five points in time (1990, 1995, 2000, 2005, and 2010).[2] Then, these percentages were pooled based on a simple average, and the mean from this calculation became the five dependent variables.[3]

Closely following the previous literature, and for reasons of parsimony, I selected the six independent variables that were the most common across studies that investigated the variation in female and/or minority office holding and that significantly predicted the presence of female and/or minority legislators: pool of potential candidates, political culture, percent of minority population, political ideology, professionalization of the state legislature, and multimember districts.

For purposes of comparability, the independent variables were measured in much the same way that other variation studies operationalize these concepts with two exceptions. First, the "pool of potential candidates" variable typically consists of three measures: the percentage of women with higher education, the percentage of professional women, and percentage of women in the workforce. To overcome any potential correlational problems associated with these indicators, my measure for this variable is the percentage of professional women in the state as identified by the U.S. Census Bureau's 1990, 2000, and 2010 Summary Files.[4] As stated in Chapter 2, because a professional career presupposes a higher education *and* workforce participation, it will most likely capture the effect of both of these indicators in one variable.

Second, political culture is cited as one of the most significant indicators for explaining the cross-sectional variation in female office holding. Although all the comparable studies attest to its predictive capacity, there is not a consistent measurement of the variable. Some studies use Elazar's categories of Moralistic and/or Traditionalistic cultures as dummy variables, others use Sharkansky's scale, and some use Johnson's scale.[5] Elazar's original typology categorized states as Moralistic, Traditionalistic, Individualistic, or a combination of two of these.[6] In order to capture the mixture designations, Sharkansky developed a scale ranging from 1 (*purely Moralistic*) to 9 (*purely Traditionalistic*).[7] Johnson developed a subculture index based on Elazar's designations through a measure of religiosity.[8] I selected Sharkansky's scale to measure political culture for this project because his index includes "mixed" cultures, which allows for a more nuanced analysis of Elazar's categories and the variations of political culture designations. If previous studies are correct, we should expect to see fewer female state legislators the closer a state gets to 9 on the scale.

The measurement of the remaining independent variables runs parallel to the other variation studies. The minority population was calculated as a percent of the nonwhite state population (black, Latino, Asian American, and Native Americans) as indicated by U.S. Census Bureau data, and I use the pooled average from these three time points.[9] Political ideology was measured using Erikson, Wright, and McIver's files, which are now appropriately updated for state-level and multi-year application.[10] They employed a 0 to 1 scale, with 0 indicating more conservative and 1 indicating more liberal. I applied Squire's scale for measuring the professionalization of the state legislature, which accounts for the time involved, resources available, and salary of state legislators.[11] The 0 (*least professional*) to 1 (*most professional*) scale is included in this analysis. For multimember districts, I created a dummy variable, where states without multimember districts are coded as 0 and states with multimember districts are coded as 1 in my data set.[12]

Finally, Palmer and Simon argue "that the partisanship of a district interacts with both the gender and the race of the candidate. In other words, minority women come from districts with different partisan leanings than white women."[13] Nelson explains that "[if] legislatures change party control from Democratic to Republican, and vice versa, this should ideally have an important effect on their party members' political fortunes."[14] Additionally, because a majority of female legislators and legislators of color (and more than 85% of women of color legislators) are Democrats, I included a control variable for party control based on Ceaser and Saldin's "major party index," which "is intended to measure the level and extent of interparty competition in and between the states" and "is comprised of six weighted components calculated on even numbered years for each state from 1990 to 2002."[15] The higher the index number, the more Republican control in the state legislature.

In the following, I relist the set of testable hypotheses that I developed in Chapter 2 for ease of interpretation. Each hypothesis comprises three parts: "a" reestablishes the conventional wisdom in the literature on the variation in women's office holding, "b" states a prediction about how the factor will apply to the variation in white women's legislative presence, and "c" predicts how I expect the factor to influence the variation of women of color legislators across the states:

H1a: States with higher levels of professional women will have higher percentages of female legislators.

H1b: States with higher levels of professional women will have higher percentages of white female legislators.

H1c: States with higher levels of professional women will have higher percentages of women of color legislators.

H2a: States with Moralistic political cultures will have higher percentages of female legislators.

H2b: States with Moralistic political cultures will have higher percentages of white female legislators.

H2c: States with Moralistic political cultures will have lower percentages of women of color legislators.

H3a: States with higher levels of liberal political ideology will have higher percentages of female legislators.

H3b: States with higher levels of liberal political ideology will have higher percentages of white female legislators.

H3c: States with higher levels of liberal political ideology will have lower percentages of women of color legislators.

H4a: States with higher percentages of minority populations will have higher percentages of female legislators.

H4b: States with higher percentages of minority populations will have lower percentages of white female legislators.

H4c: States with higher percentages of minority populations will have higher percentages of women of color legislators.

H5a: States with higher levels of legislative professionalization will have lower percentages of female legislators.

H5b: States with higher levels of legislative professionalization will have lower percentages of white female legislators

H5c: States with higher levels of legislative professionalization will have lower percentages of women of color legislators

H6a: States with multimember districts will have higher percentages of female legislators.

H6b: States with multimember districts will have higher percentages of white female legislators.

H6c: States with multimember districts will have higher percentages of women of color legislators.

RESULTS: WOMEN OF COLOR AND STATE LEGISLATIVE VARIATION

How well does the conventional wisdom about the variation in female office holding perform when applied to different groups of women legislators? Table 4.1 presents the ordinary least squares (OLS) regression coefficients (and

Table 4.1 Unstandardized Regression Coefficients (and Standard Errors) for the Percentage of Women, White Women, and Women of Color in State Legislatures

	Women	White Women	Women of Color
Percentage of Professional Women	**2.401*** (1.209)	**2.316**** (1.196)	0.115 (0.436)
Political Culture	**−0.011**** (0.005)	**−0.014***** (0.005)	**0.003*** (0.001)
Liberal Ideology	**0.696**** (0.292)	**0.716**** (0.289)	−0.047 (0.106)
Percentage of Minority Population	0.073 (0.064)	**−0.155*** (0.063)	**0.219***** (0.023)
Legislative Professionalization	−0.095 (0.063)	−0.090 (0.062)	0.001 (0.023)
Multimember Districts	**0.035**** (0.015)	**0.039**** (0.015)	−0.005 (0.005)
Constant	−0.013 (0.104)	0.044 (0.105)	0.034 (0.038)
Adjusted R^2	0.551	0.629	0.776
Sig. of Model (F-Statistic)	9.599***	12.845***	25.294***

***$p < .01$. **$p < .05$. *$p < .10$.

Note: Boldfaced coefficients are statistically significant.

standard errors) for the percentage of women, white women, and women of color in state legislatures. The first thing to note is that the model is statistically significant and performs fairly well (adjusted $R^2 = 0.551$) in explaining the variation we see in women's legislative service overall. In terms of my hypotheses, four expectations are confirmed: states with higher percentages of professional women, higher levels of liberal political ideologies, multimember districts, and those that come closer to approximating a Moralistic political culture are all significantly positive for predicting higher percentages of female state legislators. These results confirm the H1a, H2a, H3a, and H6a hypotheses.[16]

Against my expectation and the previous literature, a higher percentage of minorities within the population does not independently predict female service in this data set. Although the coefficient is positive, it is not significant. One possible reason for this could be that this variable is operationalized using aggregate state-level data. As stated earlier, measuring the minority population in this fashion may be hiding district-level characteristics. Legislative professionalization was a negative indicator of women's service as hypothesized, but not a significant factor for explaining the variation in female office holding. As such, I can neither confirm nor reject H4a or H5a.

How does the model perform when we apply an intersectional framework? I argued earlier that if we take the race/ethnicity of the legislator into account, the factors in the model would not offer the same predictive capacity as cited in previous studies. Table 4.1 offers some initial support for this argument if we consider the percentage of white women legislators and the percentage of women of color legislators for the same set of independent variables. Although both models reach statistical significance, the model better explains the variance for women of color (adjusted R^2 = 0.776) than it does for white women (adjusted R^2 = 0.629).

Assessing the results for white female legislators, most of the expectations are confirmed and support previous work in this area: states with higher levels of professional women (H1b), Moralistic political cultures (H2b), liberal ideologies (H3b), and multimember districts (H6b) have higher percentages of white women legislators, and states with *higher* levels of minority populations have *lower* levels of white female office holders (H4b). Although the result for the percentage of the minority population does not go against what I expected, this one variable does not comport with the previous literature—it is negatively related to white female service. I offer a possible explanation for this result later when I discuss women of color's service. The level of legislative professionalization is in the anticipated direction but, once more, is not statistically significant. I cannot confirm or reject H5b. In sum, four of the variables that best explain white female's presence in legislatures are similar in direction and significance to the variables that help us understand the cross-sectional variation in women legislative service overall.

Applying the same model to office holding by women of color, we see that the predictive capacity and direction of the variables in the model changes fairly substantially. Two expectations are confirmed: states with higher percentages of minority populations and states that fall closer to *Traditionalistic* political cultures tend to have higher percentages of women of color legislators, confirming H2c and H4c. I originally hypothesized that the percentage of professional women in the state would matter more for women of color than for white women. This is not the case. Although the percentage of professional women in the state has a positive effect on women of color's legislative service, it is not a significant relationship. This might be related to how women of color enter the political arena, with some studies suggesting that their path differs from that of white women.[17] It also might be related to recruitment pools. If women candidates are mainly recruited from professions such as the law and business, but women of color are underrepresented within those professions; it is possible that occupational sectors in which women of color are more prevalent are not being tapped, such as education and social work.

Liberal political ideology performs in the expected direction but does not have a significant independent effect on women of color descriptive representation. Squire found that lower levels of female office holding occurred in states with higher levels of conservative ideology.[18] But he found the opposite for black office holding. From this analysis, his finding is confirmed but is conditioned on the race/ethnicity of the woman. Less conservative political ideology in the state has a positive impact on white women, but this relationship does not hold for women of color.

Legislative professionalization for women of color legislators moves in the opposite direction of my expectations but is not significant. In his studies, Casellas found that the level of professionalization in the state legislator was only significant when it interacted with the percentage of Latino population in the state.[19] That could be a possible explanation for this unexpected finding, as I did not include interactions in my analysis. Even so, Casellas documented that *less* professionalized legislatures were more favorable to Latinos, and the positive direction for women of color in this data set indicates otherwise for women of color. Casellas's studies focused on Latinos, where I incorporated all minorities. The other thing to consider is that Casellas did not account for gender, and so his results may be picking up the effect of legislative professionalization for Latinos and not Latinas in his analysis. This last point becomes clearer later in this chapter when I look at the gender differences between legislators of color.

The presence of multimember districts for women of color legislators also goes against what I expected, but I did not find this to be a significant relationship. I discuss some possibilities for this when I assess the findings for legislators of color later. In short, H1c, H3c, H5c, and H6c cannot be accepted or rejected as independent indicators for explaining the geographical variation in the presence of women of color in state legislatures. Given that a legislator is a woman, the level of professional women in the state, liberal ideology, legislative professionalization, and multimember districts do not significantly predict that she will be a woman of color.

Recall that when we do not take the race/ethnicity of the female legislator into account, the percentage of the minority population does not perform as expected. However, when we disaggregate female legislators by race/ethnicity, this factor is negatively associated with white female legislators and positively associated with women of color legislators. This makes intuitive sense: women of color are more likely to emerge in states with higher percentages of people of color. As such, two things are particularly interesting about the preceding findings. First, the extant literature consistently confirms that higher percentages of minority populations predict higher percentages of female legislators. Perhaps this is a function of the time frames under consideration in the other studies—most were conducted at a time when we see women of color's legislative presence increasing and they could be capturing this phenomenon. Since the data for this project moves us into the 2000s, when all of women's legislative service leveled off, it is possible that my assessment notes a declining importance of this factor. Theoretically, however, the findings discussed here may confirm not the declining importance per se, but the *relative* importance of this particular variable. Indeed, higher percentages of nonwhite populations positively and significantly predict the presence of women of color legislators but negatively and significantly predict white females.

Second, the other item that goes against the previous literature but confirms my expectation is the political culture variable. Again, Moralistic political culture is one of the most reliable factors for explaining cross-sectional variation, and it does perform as expected for female legislators overall as well as white women in particular. This pattern does not hold for female legislators of color. In fact, we are more likely to see their presence as states move closer to the Traditionalistic end of the culture scale.

On one hand, a possible explanation for this finding might be related to region. Almost all southern states have Traditionalistic political cultures, and in these states, we see higher percentages of women of color in the legislature. Higher levels of white women, conversely, serve in northeastern and midwestern states, which are more likely to have Moralistic political cultures.

On the other hand, both white women and women of color have higher levels of legislative service in western states, which are typically categorized as a mix of Individualistic/Moralistic or Individualistic/Traditionalistic. Furthermore, Elazar's typology is in part based on region (namely, by attempting to explain regional differences), and Sharkansky partially controls for the inclusion of Individualistic and "mixed" states with his scaled estimations. Region, then, may not be the only mitigating factor when interpreting these results.

Keep in mind that the preceding examination of the geographical variation explains the differences among women— it offers a racial/ethnic analysis of gender. How does the model perform when applied to legislators of color? In other words, what happens when a gendered analysis of race/ethnicity is the subject at hand? For comparative purposes, I re-ran this same model with legislators of color and men of color as the dependent variables. Table 4.2 lists the OLS regression coefficients (and standard errors) for the percentage of legislators of color and men of color in state legislatures. The coefficients for women of color are represented in Table 4.2 for ease of comparison. The model is statistically significant and

112 Gender, Race, and Office Holding in the United States

Table 4.2 Unstandardized Regression Coefficients (and Standard Errors) for the Percentage of Legislators of Color, Men of Color, and Women of Color in State Legislatures

	Legislators of Color	Men of Color	Women of Color
Percentage of Professional Women	−3.125**	−3.247***	0.115
	(1.338)	(0.994)	(0.436)
Political Culture	0.008*	0.005*	0.003*
	(0.003)	(0.002)	(0.001)
Liberal Ideology	0.071	0.113	−0.047
	(0.324)	(0.240)	(0.106)
Percentage of Minority Population	0.878***	0.678***	0.219***
	(0.071)	(0.053)	(0.023)
Legislative Professionalization	−0.094	−0.092*	0.001
	(0.070)	(0.052)	(0.023)
Multimember Districts	−0.029*	−0.024*	−0.005
	(0.017)	(0.012)	(0.005)
Constant	0.144	0.112	0.034
	(0.115)	(0.086)	(0.038)
Adjusted R^2	0.839	0.844	0.776
Sig. of Model (F-Statistic)	37.478***	38.983***	25.294***

***$p < .01$. **$p < .05$. *$p < .10$.

Note: Boldfaced coefficients are statistically significant.

performs incredibly well (adjusted $R^2 = 0.839$) in explaining the variation we see in legislator of color's service overall, and is even better at explaining men of color's legislative service (adjusted $R^2 = 0.844$).[20]

In keeping with previous literature, the percentage of the minority population positively and significantly predicts higher percentages of legislators of color, regardless of gender. Also similar to what the race and ethnic politics literature would suggest is the independent effects of multimember districts—states *without* multimember districts have higher levels of legislators of color. As noted earlier, multimember districts did not have a significant impact for women of color's legislative presence, but here they do seem to be negatively and significantly associated with legislators of color overall and men of color specifically.

This result also slightly modified what we know about the intersectional effect of single versus multimember, as discussed in Chapter 2—single member districts are favorable for men of color, whereas multimember districts favor women of color.[21] While the present study does not indicate a significant relationship for women of color, the direction of the coefficient goes against what might be expected, specifying that women of color legislators may have more in common with their male counterparts than their female counterparts with regards to single or multimember districts. This finding is considered more fully in Chapter 5 when I look at proportional gender gaps.

Legislative professionalization mirrors the literature as well: states with more professional legislatures will have lower levels of legislators of color.[22] What is new about this analysis is that previous findings may be capturing the consequence that professionalization has on men of color. Within this study, the level of legislative professionalization is not a significant predictor for women of color legislators, but in the opposite hypothesized direction. In short, I conditionally confirm Casellas's results—*men* of color benefit from less professionalized legislatures.

And, contrary to what Casellas found, liberal political ideology does not have an independent influence on Latino office holding, irrespective of gender.[23] The direction of the relationship substantiates his findings, but again, this is qualified: higher percentages of men of color in states with higher levels liberal political ideology for men of color but lower percentages of women of color legislators in states with higher levels of liberal ideology. Again, this is not a significant relationship, but the direction of the coefficients give pause to previous literature in this area. For women, white women specifically, liberal ideology matters. For legislators of color, of both genders, liberal ideology does not matter. This might be due to the differences in our time frames as well as some of the differences in the dependent and independent variables with our models.[24] It could also be related to the regional differences I considered above.

Two of the variables within the model have not been tested in race and ethnic politics literature with regard to explaining geographical variation. For political culture, the more a state moves towards a Traditionalistic culture, the more legislators of color there will be in the legislature, both male and female. Although this particular iteration of the variable has not been specifically employed to address the *variation of legislators* of color across the states, the results presented here are intuitive for the reasons listed earlier when I discussed it's meaning for women of color legislators.[25]

For the second variable, the percentage of professional women within the state, there is no reason to expect that this indicator would stand out as a significant predictor of office holding by a legislator of color, especially in the direction presented here. I did not remove it in this assessment simply because I wanted to make the application of the models as consistent as possible and because it is also included in the gender gap analysis presented in Chapter 5. The results are a bit striking, though. This particular variable has a *negative* and *significant* association with the geographical variation of legislators of color in general, men of color legislators specifically, but no independent association with service by women of color. Why?

One possible reason might be linked to socioeconomic status. Some research within race and ethnic politics suggests that elected officials of color are more likely to come from districts that have lower levels of income, education, employment, and/or higher levels of poverty.[26] My measure of professional women would encapsulate those who have higher levels of socioeconomic status, at least among the female population. Therefore, the higher levels of socioeconomic status that I am capturing are predicting lower percentages of legislators of color, which does match up with what we would expect from the literature. In other words, it may be in keeping with the previous findings and explain the results presented here, but it is conditioned on the gender of the legislator of color.

Geographical Variation at the Intersection 115

All in all, both men and women of color seem to have higher percentages of legislative offices in Traditionalistic states that have higher percentages of minority population. Otherwise, the differences include the importance of less professionalized legislatures, single-member districts, and lower levels of professional women for men of color, none of which demonstrate any independent significance for women of color.

CONCLUSION: PREDICTING THE VARIATION IN OFFICE HOLDING BY WOMEN OF COLOR

The purpose of this chapter was to revisit the explanation for the variation we see in women's legislative service across the state from an intersectional framework. Applying this theoretical concept to the set of variables that have been consistently used to explain female legislator's cross-sectional variation, I tested the model's predicting capacity to determine whether these variables were the same or different when comparing white women and women of color. I then applied this same model to geographical variation in legislators of color. My analysis offers some initial support for the theory that intersection matters regarding female office holding.

The explanatory power of six independent factors under consideration here varies depending on whether female legislators are white or of color, as well as whether the legislator of color is male or female. Generally speaking, white women and women of color legislators had very little in common in terms of predictors. Likewise, women of color had very little in common with their male counterparts. Table 4.3 offers a modified version of the typology originally presented in Chapter 2, summarizing the above results.

We are more likely to see higher percentages of white female legislators in states with higher percentages of professional women, higher levels of liberal political ideologies among the electorate, multimember districts, and those classified as having a Moralistic culture. We are less likely to see white female legislators in states with higher percentages of minority populations and professionalized legislatures. Women of color

Table 4.3 Modified Typology: Predictors of Descriptive Representation at the State Level

Significant Independent Variables	Expected Levels of Representation				
	Women	White Women	Women of Color	Legislators of Color	Men of Color
Higher Percentages of Professional Women	Higher	Higher	–	Lower	Lower
Type of Political Culture	More Moralistic	More Moralistic	More Traditionalistic	More Traditionalistic	More Traditionalistic
Higher Levels of Liberal Ideology	Higher	Higher	–	–	–
Higher Percentages of Minority Population	–	–	Higher	Higher	Higher
Higher Legislative Professionalization	–	–	–	–	–
Type of Districts in the State	Multimember	Multimember	–	Single Member	Single Member

Note: A "–" in the table indicates that this variable is not a significant predictor of representation.

legislators are more likely to serve in states that fall closer to having a Traditionalistic political culture and higher percentages of minority population. Men of color have higher percentages of office holding in states with higher minority populations, Traditionalistic political cultures, lower levels of professional women, less professionalized legislatures, and single-member districts.

Speaking directly to the women and politics literature, the key idea that I would like to emphasize is that the model for explaining the geographical variation in women's legislative service more closely matches the level of service by white women legislators than in office holding by women of color. This indicates that previous findings more accurately describe white women legislator's presence and less accurately predict the proportion of women of color state legislators. Instead, the research presented here reveals that the indicators most useful in predicting women's legislative service are noticeably raced, as they are less helpful in explaining where women of color serve. In short, race/ethnicity did make a difference when I applied the model to women legislators, disaggregated by race/ethnicity, as well as when I applied the model to legislators of color, disaggregated by gender. Clearly, gender and race/ethnicity are intersecting when it comes to legislative office holding.

NOTES

1. Data collected for this project were made possible in part by Summer Research Grants from the School of Social Sciences and the Department of Political Science at the University of California, Irvine and The Office of the Provost at Saint Joseph's University.
2. The selection of the data points represents five-year intervals. The year 1990 marks a point in time in which we begin to see structural changes in state legislatures, for instance, increasing professionalization. Other years offer differing electoral contexts (i.e., 1995 represents a point in time after the 1992 "Year of the Woman" elections; 2000 was presidential election year; 2005 represents office holding after the 2000 census and, thus, redistricting changes; and the year 2010 is the most recent year for which I could collect comparable data).
3. See Chapter 3 for a complete discussion of data sources consulted for all five dependent variables.

4. United States Census Bureau, "United States Census 1990, Summary File 3," 1990, http://factfinder.census.gov/servlet/Data setMainPageServlet?_ds_name=DEC_1990_STF3_&_ program=DEC&_lang=en; United States Census Bureau, "United States Census 2000, Summary File 3," http://www.cen sus.gov/Press-Release/www/2002/sumfile3.html; and United States Census Bureau, "United States Census 2010, Summary File 2," 2010, http://www.census.gov/2010census/data.
5. See Daniel J. Elazar, *American Federalism: A View from the States* (New York: Thomas Y. Crowell Company, 1966); Kevin Arceneaux, "The 'Gender Gap' in State Legislative Representation: New Data to Tackle and Old Question," *Political Research Quarterly* 54 (2001): 143–160; Robert E. Hogan, "The Influences of State and District Conditions on the Representation of Women in U.S. State Legislatures," *American Politics Research* 29 (2001): 4–24; Ira Sharkansky, "The Utility of Elazar's Political Culture: A Research Note," *Polity* 2 (1969): 66–83; Carol Nechemias, "Changes in the Election of Women to U.S. State Legislative Seats," *Legislative Studies Quarterly* 8, no. 1 (1987): 125–142; Barbara Norrander and Clyde Wilcox, "The Geography of Gender Power: Women in State Legislatures," in *Women and Elective Office: Past, Present, and Future*, ed. Sue Thomas and Clyde Wilcox (New York: Oxford University Press, 1998), 103–117; Barbara Norrander and Clyde Wilcox, "Change in Continuity in the Geography of Women State Legislators," In *Women and Elective Office: Past, Present, and Future*, 2nd ed., ed. Sue Thomas and Clyde Wilcox (New York: Oxford University Press, 2005): 176–196; Charles A. Johnson, "Political Culture in American States: Elazar's Formulation Examined," *American Journal of Political Science* 20, no. 3 (August 1976): 491–509; David B. Hill, "Political Culture and Female Political Representation," *The Journal of Politics* 43 (1981): 159–168.
6. Daniel J. Elazar, *American Federalism: A View from the States* (New York: Thomas Y. Crowell Company, 1966); Daniel J. Elazar, *American Federalism: A View from the States*, 3rd ed. (New York: Harper Collins College Division, 1984).
7. Sharkansky, "The Utility of Elazar's Political Culture."
8. Johnson, "Political Culture in American States."
9. United States Census Bureau, "United States Census 1990"; United States Census Bureau, "United States Census 2000, Summary File 3," and United States Census Bureau, "United States Census 2010, Summary File 2."
10. Robert S. Erikson, Gerald C. Wright, and John P. McIver, "Replication Data for: Public Opinion in the States: A Quarter Century of Change and Stability," 2007, http://hdl.handle. net/1902.1/10442 UNF:3:42A1SVhk3cWA2Ss5az8zjQ.

11. Peverill Squire, "Measuring State Legislative Professionalism: The Squire Index Revisited," *State Politics and Policy Quarterly* 7, no. 2 (Summer 2007): 211–227.
12. States are coded 1 if it had multimember districts during the twenty-year span under investigation. The author understands that this is a blunt measurement of multimember districts, but given the changing nature of these districts at the state level, it was the cleanest method for capturing the presence of such districts across the two decades.
13. Barbara Palmer and Dennis Simon, *Breaking the Political Glass Ceiling: Women and Congressional Elections*, 2nd ed. (New York: Routledge, 2008), 194.
14. Albert Nelson, *Emerging Influentials in State Legislatures: Women, Blacks, and Hispanics* (Westport, CT: Praeger, 1991), 6.
15. James W. Ceaser and Robert P. Saldin, "A New Measure of Party Strength," *Political Research Quarterly* 58, no. 2 (June 2005): 247.
16. The control variable for party was not statistically significant in any of the models presented in this book. Within this study, whether a legislature was more under Democratic or Republican control did not have an independent effect on the geographical variation or the gender gaps, after controlling for all else. This could be a function of the time frame under investigation and that fact that the overwhelming majority of legislators of color are Democrats, and so are women legislators, but to a lesser extent than legislators of color. In addition, Simon and Palmer indicate that, at the congressional district level, " 'party-friendly' and 'women-friendly' are not the same concept. Women-friendly districts have their own unique political geographies." Even so, please note that this eventuality was indeed controlled for in the current study. See Palmer and Simon, *Breaking the Political Glass Ceiling*, 199.
17. Gary Moncrief, Joel Thompson, and Robert Schuhmann, "Gender, Race, and the State Legislature: A Research Note on the Double Disadvantage Hypothesis," *Social Science Journal* 28 (1991): 481–87; Linda Faye Williams, "The Civil Rights-Black Power Legacy: Black Women Elected Officials at the Local, State, and National Levels," in *Sisters in the Struggle: African American Women in the Civil Rights-Black Power Movement*, ed. Bettye Collier-Thomas and V.P. Franklin (New York: New York University Press, 2001), 306–331; and Paule Cruz Takash, "Breaking Barriers to Representation: Chicana/Latina Elected Officials in California" in *Women Transforming Politics: An Alternative Reader*, ed. by Cathy J. Cohen, Kathleen B. Jones, and Joan C. Tronto (New York: New York University Press, 1997), 412–434.

18. Peverill Squire, "Legislative Professionalization and Membership Diversity in State Legislatures," *Legislative Studies Quarterly* 17, no. 1 (February 1992): 69–79.
19. Jason P. Casellas, "The Institutional and Demographic Determinants of Latino Representation," *Legislative Studies Quarterly* 34, no. 3 (Aug. 2009): 399–425; and Jason Casellas, *Latino Representation in State Houses and Congress* (Cambridge: Cambridge University Press, 2011).
20. The author acknowledges that the R^2 for the legislator of color and men of color models are quite high, but that most of the coefficients are not. To allow for the possibility of collinearity, I reran the models with only the significant variables to see if the R^2 decreased, which would indicate that some combination of the variables was explaining my results. However, the R^2 for these condensed models was still quite high (0.783 and 0.799, respectively), meaning that the significant coefficients really are doing all of the work in explaining the variation in office holding for both groups.
21. Robert Darcy, Charles D. Hadley, and Jason F. Kirksey, "Election Systems and the Representation of Black Women in American State Legislatures," *Women & Politics* 13, no. 2 (1993): 73–89; Bernard Grofman and Lisa Handley, "The Impact of the Voting Rights Act on Black Representation in Southern State Legislatures," *Legislative Studies Quarterly* 16, no. 1 (February 1991): 111–128; Gary F. Moncrief and Joel A. Thompson, "Electoral Structures and State Legislative Representation: A Research Note," *Journal of Politics* 54, no. 1 (February 1992): 246–256; and Wilma Rule, "Multimember Legislative Districts: Minority and Anglo Women's and Men's Recruitment Opportunity," in *United States Electoral Systems: Their Impact on Women and Minorities*, ed. Wilma Rule and Joseph F. Zimmerman (Westport, CT: Praeger, 1992), 57–72.
22. Casellas, "The Institutional and Demographic Determinants"; and Casellas, *Latino Representation*.
23. Casellas, *Latino Representation*.
24. Casellas looked at presidential years (1992, 1996, 2000, and 2004). For the dependent variable, he focused specifically on Latino state legislators. For the independent variables, his study included the percent Latino in the state, and he also accounted for term limits. See Casellas, *Latino Representation*.
25. Although see Fitzpatrick and Hero, who tested "the relationships between Elazar's construct of political culture and several characteristics of the political behavior, structure, processes and outcomes in the American states." Jody L. Fitzpatrick and Rodney E. Hero, "Political Culture and Political

Characteristics of the American States: A Consideration of Some Old and New Questions," *Western Political Quarterly* 41, no. 1 (March 1988): 146.

They found that "Moralistic states tended to have more party competition . . . [and] made greater use of merit systems than did individualistic or traditionalistic states . . . Moralistic states [also] demonstrate greater policy innovation and greater economic equality among its citizens." See Fitzpatrick and Hero, "Political Culture." Even so, these authors did not look at how their findings have had an impact on the presence of a legislator of color. Also see Rodney E. Hero and Caroline J. Tolbert, "Racial/Ethnic Diversity Interpretation of Politics and Policy in the States of the U.S.," *American Journal of Political Science* 40, no. 3 (August 1996): 851–871; and Rodney Hero, *Faces of Inequality: Social Diversity in American Politics* (Oxford University Press, 1998) for an in-depth look at how political culture is related to inequality, minority population density, and regional variations.

26. James Button and David Hedge, "Legislative Life in the 1990s: A Comparison of Black and White State Legislators," *Legislative Studies Quarterly* 21, no. 2, (May 1996): 199–218; Kerry Haynie, *African American State Legislators in the American States* (New York: Columbia University Press, 2001); Palmer and Simon, *Breaking the Political Glass Ceiling*; James W. Endersby and Charles E. Menifield, "Representation, Ethnicity, and Congress: Black and Hispanic Representatives and Constituencies," in *Black and Multiracial Politics in America*, ed. Yvette M. Alex-Assensoh and Lawrence J. Hanks (New York: New York University Press, 2000), 257–272; Thomas E. Cavanagh and Denise Stockton, *Black Elected Officials and their Constituencies* (Washington, DC: Joint Center for Political Studies, 1983); Albert K. Karing and Susan Welch, "Sex and Ethnic Differences in Municipal Representation," *Social Science Quarterly* 60, no. 3 (December 1979): 465–480; and Charles S. Bullock, "The Election of Blacks in the South: Preconditions and Consequences," *American Journal of Political Science* 19, no. 4 (November 1975): 727–739.

5 Gender Gaps at the Intersection

In the last chapter, I discussed the question of variation of female legislators across the states and determined that the model derived from the conventional wisdom does fairly well in explaining where women, in general, and white women will serve. In other words, given that a female legislator is present, what has an impact on the likelihood that she will be white or of color? The model also explains where legislators of color in general and men of color are more likely to be present across the states. However, this same specification of the variables does not equally apply to the variation in women of color's legislative service. The only two state-level predictors that women of color have in common with their male counterparts are political culture (more Traditionalistic states) and higher percentages of minority populations within the state. In terms of significance, women of color share these same predictors with white female legislators as well, but the relationship is in the opposite direction for both coefficients.[1] Regarding geographical variation, then, this initial set of evidence suggests that race trumps gender as a politically relevant characteristic. Women of color are more like their male counterparts with regards to geographical variation in state legislative service.

Assessing the variation, however, does not necessarily explain why women of color serve at proportionally higher rates than do white female legislators. It helps for understanding *where* we are more or less likely to see women of color in state legislatures overall, but not *why* there is a lower gender gap among legislators of color compared to white legislators. Recall from Chapter 3 that in state legislative office holding, the gender gap among legislators of color is much smaller than the gender gap among whites, even within the same state. However, states where women of color have the highest levels of service are also the states where the legislator of color gender gap is the highest. Considering that the percentage of the minority population within a state is one of the two significant predictors of women of color's office holding, then why are the largest gender gaps in legislators of color also present within these *same states*? Gender, therefore, is a politically relevant characteristic for women of color, and it clearly influences state legislative service. If it did not inform office holding, then we would see equal numbers of men and women of color in our state legislatures. What state-level factors explain this phenomenon? Does gender trump race regarding legislators of color?

This chapter assesses the second research question under investigation in this manuscript and offers a gendered analysis of race/ethnicity by exploring the smaller gender gap in legislator of color's office holding. Specifically, I examine how race intersects with gender by concentrating on white women and women of color as a proportion of their respective racial/ethnic group. In short, given that a legislator is white, what contexts predict that it will be a female; and given that a legislator is of color, what contexts predict that it will be a female? Using the same theoretical framework and the same set of independent variables specified in Chapter 4, I test whether or not the conventional model can be applied to the differential gender gap in office holding between white legislators and legislators of color.

EXPLAINING THE SMALLER RACIAL/ETHNIC GENDER GAP

As discussed in Chapter 3, my measure of the gender gap is the pooled average of the difference across the five points in time of interest (1990, 1995, 2000, 2005, and 2010) between the percentage of males and females in the legislature, disaggregated by race/ethnicity (white legislators and legislators of color). Negative numbers in the data set indicate that women serve at higher rates than men. The same six independent variables employed in Chapter 4 also guide this chapter: percentage of professional women in the state, political culture, liberal ideology, percentage of the minority population in the state, level of legislative professionalization, and the presence of multimember districts.[2]

Table 5.1 lists the ordinary least squares (OLS) regression coefficients (and standard errors) for the white gender gap and the legislator of color gender gap. Both models are statistically significant and perform moderately well in explaining the white gender gap (adjusted $R^2 = 0.535$) and even

Table 5.1 Unstandardized Regression Coefficients (and Standard Errors) for the White and Legislator of Color Gender Gap in State Legislatures

	White Gender Gap	Legislator of Color Gender Gap
Percentage of Professional Women	−3.373	−3.378***
	(2.753)	(0.778)
Political Culture	0.029***	−0.005*
	(0.008)	(0.002)
Liberal Ideology	**−1.701****	0.155
	(0.666)	(0.188)
Percentage of Minority Population	−0.152	0.460***
	(0.146)	(0.041)
Legislative Professionalization	0.272*	−0.095**
	(0.143)	(0.040)
Multimember Districts	−0.076**	−0.019*
	(0.034)	(0.010)
Control: Rep Party Control	−0.291	−0.051
	(0.239)	(0.068)
Constant	1.048	0.080
	(0.237)	(0.067)
Adjusted R^2	0.535	0.796
Sig. of Model (F-Statistic)	9.039***	28.328***

***p < .01. **p < .05. *p < .10.

Note: Boldfaced coefficients are statistically significant.

better at explaining legislator of color gender gap (adjusted $R^2 = 0.796$). Keep in mind that the dependent variable is the gender gap, meaning that a positive coefficient indicates an *increase* in the gender gap and a negative coefficient designates a *decrease* in the gender gap.

What explains the white gender gap in office holding? The results in Table 5.1 indicate that there is a higher gender gap in white office holding in states with Traditionalistic political cultures and more professionalized legislatures. As a state moves closer to Traditionalistic on the political culture scale and the more professionalized a legislature is within the state, the white gender gap increases—there is less parity between white men and women. Conversely, as the level of liberal political ideology increases in a state, the white gender gap goes down—there is more parity between white men and women. States that have multimember districts also result in smaller white gender gaps.

Although in Chapter 4, the higher percentages of professional women and the lower percentages of minority populations in the state were both significantly associated with higher level of white women's legislative presence, neither of these variables independently explains the *proportional* gender composition of white legislators across the states. This implies that the factors that best explain the *variation* of white women across states, measured as their percentage of the total legislature, do not necessarily predict their *parity* with men *within the same state*, measured as their proportion of whites within the legislature.

Turning to the legislator of color gender gap, the results in Table 5.1 suggest that the gender gap goes *down* in states with higher percentages of professional women, more Traditionalistic political cultures, less professionalized legislatures, and multimember districts. The legislator of color gender gap *goes up* in states with higher percentages of minority populations. Liberal ideology does not significantly explain the legislator of color gender gap. In Chapter 4, I illustrated that only two variables, political culture and minority population, predicted the variation in office holding by women of color. Both were positive and significant. Whereas Traditionalistic political cultures still seem to influence the descriptive representation of women of color, the percentage of the minority population is *inversely* related.

This finding adds weight to the observation I made earlier and in Chapter 3 about the legislator of gender gap being highest in states with higher minority populations. In other words, the chances that a legislator will be of color increases as the minority population increases, as the variation models in Chapter 4 document. *But the chances that that legislator of color will be a woman decrease as the minority population increases*, as the gender gap model specifies in the current chapter. Hawaii is a perfect example of this scenario. It is the state with the highest minority population, yet it is also the state with the highest racial/ethnic gender gap. It also has one of the lowest white gender gaps, with white women represent 44.9% of all white legislators on average. The same can be said of New Mexico, where Latinas are responsible for a majority of the growth in Latino representation in the state but still experience one of the highest legislator of color gender gaps. Why?

Here, the other variables in the model might help to account for this effect. The percentage of professional women, level of legislative professionalization, and multimember districts were not significantly related to women of color's geographical variation, but all three predicted where men of color would serve. However, in the gender gap model earlier, they are statistically significant predictors of the legislator of color gender gap. Hence, after controlling for the state's minority population, women of color increase their descriptive representation within their racial/ethnic group in states with higher percentages of professional women, multimember districts, and *more* professionalized legislatures. This last finding is discussed further later in this chapter.

The result for multimember districts is in line with previous studies for both the white and legislator of color gender gap, and was also a significant variable for understanding the geographical variation in women, but white women specifically.[3] So, in terms of the geographical variation, the presence of multimember districts did not seem to mirror previous literature. However, for explaining the proportional gender gap, the results are in line with what Darcy, Hadley, and Kirksey and Rule found in their studies: multimember districts are favorable for women, regardless of color, and single-member districts favor men of color.[4]

The percentage of professional women and the level of legislative professionalization, however, offer some curious discoveries. First, in Chapter 4, the percentage of professional women within the state positively and significantly predicted the presence of white women within state legislatures, but not women of color. To say it another way, given that a legislator was a *woman*, chances that she was a *white* woman increased as the percent of professional women in the state increased, as confirmed by the geographical variation model in Chapter 4. The level of professional women in the state did not significantly predict that the woman would be a woman of color.[5] Within the white gender gap model, however, given that a legislator is *white*, higher percentages of professional women in the state does not have an impact on the chances that it will be a *woman*. This could simply be a function of relative preparedness, with previous scholars documenting the higher levels of education among women of color legislators compared to white female legislators.[6]

In Chapter 4, within a professionalized legislature, the likelihood that a female legislator will be a white woman was not a statistically significant association. But, here, and in keeping with the extant literature, the likelihood that a white legislator is female decreases as professionalization in the legislature increases. This relationship reverses, however, for women of color. More professionalized legislatures increase the likelihood that a legislator of color will be a woman, as will higher levels of professional women within the state, a finding that goes against expectations from both the women and politics and the race and ethnic politics literature. Chapter 2 noted that scholars in both literatures suggested that states with highly professionalized legislatures were not conducive to the election of women *or* minorities.[7]

The preceding findings make this conclusion suspect or, at the very least, conditional. Within this study, the level of legislative professionalization did not effectively forecast whether a legislator will be a woman or, given that she is a woman, whether she will be white or of color. Nevertheless, it does appear to significantly estimate whether a white legislator or a legislator of color will be a female. When controlling for the race/ethnicity of the legislator, less professionalized legislative environments are more favorable for white women, and more professionalized legislatures are more favorable for women of color. It is entirely possible that the women and politics literature was picking up the effect for white women, and the race and ethnic politics literature was estimating the effect on men of color. As the current study demonstrates, more professionalized legislatures seem more favorable environments for women of color legislators as a proportion of their racial/ethnic group.

INTERSECTIONAL MODELS OF REPRESENTATION

Considering the results of the models in both Chapter 4 and this chapter, Table 5.2 offers a presentation of state environments that are more or less favorable for women, white women, and women of color that is broken down by what the geographical variation models suggest as well as by what is advised by the gender gap models.

To summarize, higher percentages of professional women within the state increase the likelihood that a female legislator will be white and that a legislator of color will be a female. Moralistic political cultures expand the possibility that a woman within the legislature will be white as well as that a white legislator will be female. More Traditionalistic political cultures, conversely, assist in estimating that a female legislator will be of color, and that a legislator of color will be a woman. Higher levels of liberal political ideology within the state predict more white women within the legislature on the whole, and more women among white legislators specifically. Higher percentages of minority populations within a state effectively estimate that a legislature will have more women of color, but decrease the likelihood that a legislator of color will be a woman. More professionalized legislatures forecast decreased numbers of women among white legislators, but increased numbers of women of color among legislators of color. Multimember districts within a state predict

Table 5.2 Combined Gender Gap and Geographical Variation Typology: Predictors of Women's State-Level Descriptive Representation

Significant Independent Variables	Geographical Variation				Racial/Ethnic Gender Gap	
	Legislature will have more women	Legislature will have more white women	Legislature will have more women of color	White legislator will be a women	Legislator of color will be a women
Higher Percentages of Professional Women	Yes	Yes	–	–	Yes
Type of Political Culture	More Moralistic	More Moralistic	More Traditionalistic	More Moralistic	More Traditionalistic
Higher Levels of Liberal Ideology	Higher	Yes	–	Yes	–
Higher Percentages of Minority Population	–	–	Yes	–	No
Higher Legislative Professionalization	–	–	–	No	Yes
Multimember Districts in the State	Yes	Yes	–	Yes	Yes

more women of all colors, both within the legislature as a whole and within their respective racial/ethnic group as well.

The analyses in Chapter 4 and this chapter offer fairly compelling evidence that gender and race/ethnicity are intersecting at the state level. What we know within the women and politics literature should be understood as conditioned by race/ethnicity—it more aptly describes the experience of white women—and what we know from the race and ethnic politics literature should be understood as conditioned by gender—it more accurately describes the experience of men of color. My evaluation of state-level environments is comparable to what Palmer and Simon found in relation to "women-friendly" congressional districts: *where* women of color serve is a function of both their gender and their race/ethnicity.[8]

NOTES

1. See Table 4.3 in Chapter 4 for a summary of these relationships.
2. A control variable for party strength is included as well. See Chapter 4 for a description of how this as well as all of the other six variables are measured.
3. See Wilma Rule, "Why More Women Are State Legislators: A Research Note," *Western Political Quarterly* 43, no. 2 (1990): 432–448; Wilma Rule, "Why Are More Women State Legislators?" in *Women in Politics: Outsiders or Insiders?*, 3rd ed., ed. Lois Duke Whitaker (Upper Saddle River, NJ: Prentice Hall, 1999): 190–201; Kevin Arceneaux, "The 'Gender Gap' in State Legislative Representation: New Data to Tackle and Old Question," *Political Research Quarterly* 54 (2001): 143–160; Albert Nelson, *Emerging Influentials in State Legislatures: Women, Blacks, and Hispanics* (Westport, CT: Praeger, 1991); Robert Darcy, Charles D. Hadley, and Jason F. Kirksey, "Election Systems and the Representation of Black Women in American State Legislatures," *Women & Politics* 13, no. 2 (1993): 73–89; Bernard Grofman and Lisa Handley, "The Impact of the Voting Rights Act on Black Representation in Southern State Legislatures," *Legislative Studies Quarterly* 16, no. 1 (February 1991): 111–128; Gary F. Moncrief and Joel A. Thompson, "Electoral Structures and State Legislative Representation: A Research Note," *Journal of Politics* 54, no. 1 (February 1992): 246–256; Anita Pritchard, "Changes in Electoral Structures and the Success of Women Candidates: The Case of

Florida," *Social Science Quarterly* 73, no. 1 (1992): 62–70; Wilma Rule, "Multimember Legislative Districts: Minority and Anglo Women's and Men's Recruitment Opportunity," in *United States Electoral Systems: Their Impact on Women and Minorities*, ed. Wilma Rule and Joseph F. Zimmerman (Westport, CT: Praeger, 1992), 57–72; and Michelle Saint-Germain, "Patterns of Legislative Opportunity in Arizona: Sex, Race, and Ethnicity," in *The Impact of U.S. Electoral Systems on Minorities and Women*, ed. W. Rule and J.F. Zimmerman (Westport: CT: Greenwood Press, 1992): 119–128.

4. Darcy, Hadley, and Kirksey, "Election Systems"; and Rule, "Multimember Legislative Districts."

5. The percentage of professional women *did* predict whether a male legislator would be a man of color, with lower percentages of professional women predicting higher levels of men of color legislators.

6. Linda Faye Williams, "The Civil Rights-Black Power Legacy: Black Women Elected Officials at the Local, State, and National Levels," in *Sisters in the Struggle: African American Women in the Civil Rights-Black Power Movement*, ed. Bettye Collier-Thomas and V.P. Franklin (New York: New York University Press, 2001), 306–331; Jewel Prestage, "Black Women State Legislators: A Profile," in *A Portrait of Marginality: The Political Behavior of the American Woman*, ed. M. Githens and J.L. Prestage (New York: David McKay, 1977), 400–418; Robert Darcy and Charles D. Hadley, "Black Women in Politics: The Puzzle Of Success," *Social Science Quarterly* 69, no. 3 (September 1988): 629–645; Gary Moncrief, Joel Thompson, and Robert Schuhmann, "Gender, Race, and the State Legislature: A Research Note on the Double Disadvantage Hypothesis," *Social Science Journal* 28 (1991): 481–87.

7. Jason Casellas, *Latino Representation in State Houses and Congress* (Cambridge: Cambridge University Press, 2011); Jason P. Casellas, "The Institutional and Demographic Determinants of Latino Representation," *Legislative Studies Quarterly* 34, no. 3 (August 2009): 399–425; David B. Hill, "Political Culture and Female Political Representation," *The Journal of Politics* 43 (1981): 159–168; Carol Nechemias, "Changes in the Election of Women to U.S. State Legislative Seats," *Legislative Studies Quarterly* 8, no. 1 (1987): 125–142; Arceneaux, "The 'Gender Gap' "; and Hogan, "The Influences of State and District Conditions."

8. Palmer and Simon, *Breaking the Political Glass Ceiling*; and Barbara Palmer and Dennis Simon, *Women and Congressional Elections: A Century of Change* (Boulder, CO: Lynne Rienner Publishers, 2012).

6 Conclusion
Representation at the Intersections

In the previous chapters, I introduced the reader to goals of the project and illustrated the puzzles under investigation: the geographical variation in state legislative service by women of color as well as the smaller racial/ethnic gender gap in office holding. The aim was to test the conventional wisdom within the women and politics literature about the geographical variation in women's office holding across the states. I suggested that applying an intersectional framework to the empirical phenomenon of women of color serving at proportionally higher rates than their white female counterparts will allow a more nuanced understanding of women's descriptive representation at the state level.

In Chapter 2, the theoretical arguments, hypotheses, and expectations were laid out. I discussed the theory of intersectionality, offered a critical analysis of the women and politics scholarship on the women legislator's geographical variation, and addressed the relevant studies from the race and ethnic politics literature. Carefully following the literature, I developed a typology as well as a set of testable hypotheses to specify the state-level conditions that might be more or less favorable for women of color's legislative service including the pool of female candidates, the state's political culture, levels of liberal political ideologies, percent of the minority population, legislative professionalization, and multimember districts.

In Chapter 3, I provided a descriptive picture of the geographical landscape and illustrated the puzzles under investigation. I presented data on where women, white women, women of color, legislators of color, and men of color served, as well as how their proportions had increased and decreased from 1990 to 2010. This analysis showed that women of color legislators tended to cluster in certain states, that women of color legislator's geographic variation did not perfectly emulate women *or* minority office holding, and that the white and legislator of color gender gaps in office holding was not uniform across the states.

Chapter 4 tested the first research question and offered a racial/ethnic analysis of gender. Given the geographical variation in women state legislators, what are the chances that a female legislator will be a woman of color? Utilizing data from a twenty-year span, my evaluation revealed that race/ethnicity intersected with gender in terms of state legislative office holding. The conventional wisdom about where women are more or less likely to serve better described white women's legislative service. Only the percentage of minority population and political culture significantly predicted the geographical variation of women of color at the state level.

Chapter 5 concentrated on the second research question and presented a gendered analysis of race/ethnicity by focusing on the smaller racial/ethnic gender gap in office holding. Given the geographical variation in service legislators of color, what are the chances that a legislator of color will be a woman? Explanations for the white gender gap and the legislator of color gender gap differed significantly. The white gender gap was lower in states with Moralistic cultures, liberal ideologies, less professionalized legislatures, and multimember districts. The legislator of color gender gap decreased in states with more professional women, Traditionalistic cultures, multimember districts, *more* professionalized legislatures, and *lower* percentages of minority populations.

If we put women of color legislators at the center of analysis, state legislative office holding is clearly both raced and gendered. The intersection of both identities influences the descriptive representational patterns of women of color. Does the conventional wisdom from the women and politics as well as from the race and ethnic politics literature apply to the case of women of color legislators? Does it help us to understand the smaller gender gap in office holding among legislators of color? Yes and no. The intersectional analysis undertaken in this book amends the conventional approaches used to account for women's office holding at the state level.

Within the current study, the conventional wisdom does not apply equally to white women and women of color when investigating the geographical variation of female legislators. The model more accurately predicts the variation in white women's and men of color's legislative service. Given that a legislator is a woman, the chances that she will be a white woman are better explained when compared to explanations for when she will be a woman of color. On the other hand, the model does much better in terms of illuminating why legislators of color have a smaller gender gap in office holding as compared to white legislators. Given that a legislator is white or of color, there are divergent reasons for forecasting when she will be a woman.[1]

Keep in mind that the aim of this book was quite simple: to test *one* set of assumptions within the women and politics literature using an intersectional analysis. To be sure, I have not even scratched the surface and have raised more questions than I have perhaps answered. For example, although I offered a summary typology of indicators that would be more or less "women-friendly" and talked about how these factors differed for white women and for women of color, I could say little, given the data I have, about how each element functions within a specific state. Table 5.2 in Chapter 5 lists some conditions for predicting *where* women, white women, and women of color are more likely to be presents, but *why* these processes would diverge across states would be better served through a state-specific analysis, not unlike Fraga et al.'s case study.[2] In short, the data here allow me to talk about state environments in general, but the reader should be careful about making assumptions about how state-level data might apply to other contexts.[3] As noted before, district-level data would more accurately describe the process of how, why, and when state-level characteristics operate.

Also suggested before is the fact that further disaggregating the data by race/ethnicity would undoubtedly offer a much more thorough understanding of office holding by women of color. Collapsing all women of color into one dependent variable is obscuring some of the processes that

136 *Gender, Race, and Office Holding in the United States*

are occurring. Indeed, running separate models for African American women, Latinas, Asian American, and Native American women, as data and numbers permit, would provide a richer story of how gender, race, and ethnicity influence legislative service. Nonetheless, what is offered in this study is basic substantiation for the contention that gender and race/ethnicity *are* intersecting for women state legislators. Moving forward, these findings should modify theories within the literature on women and politics concerning the state-level contexts that influence gender and office holding.

RETHINKING GEOGRAPHICAL VARIATION AND GENDER GAPS AT THE STATE LEVEL

Some of the more curious results for explaining the white and legislator of color gender gap revealed themselves in Chapter 5, especially in relation to office holding by women of color: the percentage of the minority population in the state and the case of multimember districts. In the following, I offer some thoughts as to the direction the literature might take in untangling these unexpected outcomes.

Minority Populations

First, the inverse relationship between the legislator of color gender gap and the percent of the minority population is truly thought-provoking. For instance, and as previously noted, in some states, the effect of race/ethnicity is reduced whereas the effect of gender is amplified. In states where legislators of color are a small portion of the total legislature, women of color are the ones who hold these seats. Conversely, in states where legislators of color compose a larger percentage of the total legislature, there is decrease in women of color's share of these seats. The same can be said for white women: the proportion of white women increases in states with low white representation and decreases in states with high white representation. But, in legislatures where racial/ethnic proportions are roughly parallel, both groups of women hold a corresponding proportion of seats. For women of color especially, the intersection of race/ethnic and gender are inversely related: when they are present in legislatures with higher levels of racial/ethnic diversity, their gender is a disadvantage; when they are present in legislatures with lower levels of racial/ethnic diversity, their gender is an advantage. Why this might be the case is severely underexplored.

One possible explanation for the lower racial/ethnic gender gap in legislatures with lower levels of diversity might be linked to their electoral base. Takash found in her survey of Latina office holders in California that "although 60.3 percent reported having majority Latino constituencies, 74.2 percent are dependent on white voting electorates."[4] Tate argues that although "[b]lack women candidates can more likely depend on their base of support coming from African American voters than can white women candidates," they also "may be better able to mobilize women voters as a whole across racial barriers."[5] Whereas this might be the case, that women of color candidates can, and do, find support within the white electorate more so than do their male counterparts, why they are emerging in particular states is left unanswered. Moreover, why they would be more likely to run for office in states with less racial/ethnic diversity is speculative as well. Part of the story is unquestionably linked to ambition (addressed below), but how do the institutional and contextual features of a state influence this clearly gendered phenomenon among legislators of color?

Multimember Districts

Several scholars have argued that "the single most important fact that explains the higher percentage of Black women serving in the U.S. Congress is the new opportunities created by the Voting Rights Act in providing new majority-Black districts from which to run."[6] In Chapter 2, I explained why I decided to utilize multimember districts to capture the effects of the Voter Rights Act (VRA). Multimember districts were eliminated and replaced with single member districts partially in response to black vote dilution and, therefore, not entirely incorrect for assessing the increase in minority office holding.

Although this might not be the ideal way to account for provisions emanating from the VRA, in this study, multimember districts are one thing that both white women and women of color have in common—multimember districts positively explain both the white and legislator of color gender gap, and this is even after controlling for the percent of the minority population in the state. Although my analysis of the gender gap clearly indicates that multimember districts influence the descriptive representation at the state level, it does not indicate that this particular feature is an advantage for women of color and *not* white women. In their study of municipal-level offices, Karnig and Welch also lament "the inability of black women to benefit from the factors which favorably influence the representation of black men."[7] Indeed, both groups of women seem to benefit from my measurement of the VRA implications. If single-member districts were created as a response to VRA regulations regarding minority vote dilution, then these changes have not seemed to benefit women of color. They do, however, benefit men of color. It will be interesting to see how this plays out now that the Supreme Court has removed much of the bite from this historic piece of legislation.

OTHER PROCESSES WORTH CONSIDERING

One would be hard-pressed to argue these days that biologically, women are not politically inclined. The evidence of women voting at higher rates than men also makes this argument suspect. But gender still seems to be a politically relevant characteristic. If biology is not the reason for the gendered discrepancies we see in political behavior, and the pool of possible women candidates is higher than ever (women's socioeconomic status has steadily increased over time and they are outpacing men in the area of education attainment), then perhaps there is a larger social or institutional process at work. If there was nothing biased about the process of becoming an elected official, then we would see no gender bias in the percentage of elected officials.

Two streams of thought in the women and politics literature attempt to explain the low levels of women office holders in the United States. The first stream relates to the institutional and contextual reasons for the disparity and attempts to identify the particular features within a state or a district environment that are more or less conducive for the election of women, the current study being one example. The second stream focuses on individual and socialization processes. It is conceivable that the reason we see fewer women running for political office is simply because women are less interested in and feel less connected to politics on the whole. Burns, Schlozman, and Brady posit that one explanation for this disconnect is that politics looks like a man's game.[8] Men, primarily white men, have dominated political arenas, especially in regards to elected office. Perhaps women have responded to this cue—women do not see other women participating, and therefore do not feel as if politics is for them.[9] This has led some scholars to suggest that the crux of the problem is that *women do not run*.[10] But how does this suggestion apply to women of color?

Ambition

Tate suggests that there is "limited evidence suggest[ing] that Black women are more inclined to run for political office than are White women."[11] Indeed, Darcy and Hadley conclude from their study of black and white women Democratic delegates that "the [greater] electoral success of black women appears to be their greater political ambition derived from their having more politically relevant backgrounds such as participation in the long civil rights struggle."[12] Of course, as Moncrief, Thompson, and Schuhmann argue that looking at women of any color who are already hold political office may not be the best method for assessing political ambition.[13] Holding political office *presupposes* ambition. Measuring differences in ambition *before* election to office is the better place to start.

When, where, and why women *do not* run for legislative office is a difficult question to answer, mainly because the empirical evidence of women who entertained the idea of running for office but then decided not run is challenging to collect given the time and resources available to political scientists. This task is further complicated from an intersectional perspective. Nevertheless, drawing on surveys and interviews with people present in traditional recruitment pools (lawyers, business owners, and others), Lawless and Fox and Lawless found that women of all colors within these groups are much less politically ambitious: "Although black and Latino eligible candidates are as likely as their white counterparts, at least at the aggregate level, to report having considered running for office, the gender gap in political ambition persists across racial and ethnic lines."[14] Lawless and Lawless and Fox did report gender differences in political ambition among racial/ ethnic groups, but it is less clear as to whether these authors looked at racial/ethnic differences *among women*.[15]

Why might women of color have more ambition than white women? Williams claims that "this heightened political ambition is attributed to: (1) socioeconomic factors; (2) double or triple consciousness as a result of race, gender, and class oppression; and (3) legacies of participatory modes developed or expanded in the Civil Rights-Black Power Era."[16] In terms of socioeconomic factors, women of color elected officials have different backgrounds characteristics compared to white women. For instance, women of color legislators have higher levels of education than do their white female counterparts.[17]

Again, however, in terms of differences in political ambition, looking only at women who have already been elected only goes so far and does not tap the initial decision to run for office. Even so, most studies that explore political ambition at the pre-candidacy level may not be capturing women of color's experience due to their focus on the legal and business professions. For example, limited evidence suggests that candidates of color emerge from arenas that are not often tapped in studies on ambition. Takash's study of Latina office holders in California indicated that the vast majority (64%) had not held previous political office and that most worked in professions such as education social work, outside of law and business.[18] Button and Hedge, in their 1991–1992 nationwide survey of black and white state legislators, claim that "a much larger percentage of [black] lawmakers are educators (20% versus 9%)" when compared to whites in their sample.[19] These authors also state that "African Americans are much more likely to report that they began their political careers outside of government, such as in the civil rights movement (50%), the church (28%), and unions (11%)."[20] Geron and Lai's survey of Latino and Asian American elected officials documented this trend, at least for Asian American elected officials: "The majority of the AAEO respondents (68.7 percent) answered that they had not held an elected position prior to their current position."[21] Regardless of background characteristics or the channels from which women of color are more likely to emerge, Perkins maintains that women of color are more likely to utilize these resources differently than white women.[22] He determines that "socialization and attitude variables are on the whole stronger correlates of ambition among black than white women ... [and that] black women *make more of the resources* in the sense that their background and attitude characteristics are closely linked to ambition."[23] Garcia and Marquez note that the Latina political elites in their analysis turn their "experiences from community-based politics, their cultural networks and resources, as well as their unique vision of politics" into political opportunities.[24] Tate makes the case that heightened political ambition among black women might partly be attributed to their having "a much longer tradition of simultaneously working and raising families. Thus, sex-role expectations may have a less dampening effect on Black women's political ambition."[25] These findings may be related to the "double or triple consciousness" noted by Williams—the idea that what at first appears to be a disadvantage can be transformed into an advantage and the necessity of having to create alternatives avenues of political power.[26]

Both of these combined, differences in the leveraging of resources and socialization experiences perhaps stem from the legacy of the Civil Rights movement, as others have suggested.[27] For instance, Clawson and Clark advise that "[i]n the case of black females, the civil rights movement, the women's movement, and the black church all contributed to the development of new party activists."[28] Nevertheless, this remains an underexplored area of research in terms of how, empirically, these processes relate *directly* to political ambition among women of color and how it varies from white women's political ambition. Two exceptions to this observation are Moore and Frederick.[29] Moore's article explores political ambition at the local (neighborhood) level and reveals that "ambition is racialized. Education increases ambition for white women. Conservative religious views increase minority women's ambition while suppressing it among white women."[30] Frederick's interviews with female candidates in Texas "find[s] that women tell quite different narratives about their decision to run for office, with Black women and Latinas expressing more confidence and self-direction in their stories than white women."[31]

Do these conclusions also hold beyond the neighborhood level and different locales? Similarly, do we see less ambitious women in certain states more than in others, and how does this vary by race/ethnicity? In other words, if the issue is one of potential female candidates, but we see a variation in women's office holding across the states as well as a smaller racial/ethnic gender gap, can it be concluded that, in some states, women are more likely to throw their hat in the electoral ring and that women of color are more inclined to do so when compared to white women? Additionally, does the mantra "when women run, they win" apply to women of color? If so, in which states? The same states that have institutional and contextual factors that are more favorable to women of color?

Political Parties

One factor that interacts with ambition and helps to determine the slate of candidates for which the electorate will vote is political parties. Sanbonmatsu explains that political party structures influence where women are more or less likely to run.[32] Some states have more open party structures and other have more closed organizations. Party gatekeepers can both keep women out and bring women in. How this varies by the race/ethnicity of the potential female candidate is not addressed.

Do strong parties matter for candidates of color? The evidence here is mixed. Cavanagh and Stockton suggest that strong party organization decrease black legislative representation.³³ Moncrief, Squire, and Jewell also found in their survey of nonincumbent state legislative candidates (1997–1998) in eight states that "[o]nly 16 percent of African-American candidates . . . report being encouraged to run by local party officials. In contrast, 48 percent of white candidates say local party leaders asked them to make the race."³⁴ They conclude that "party agents are not important recruiters in bringing African Americans to run for the state legislature."³⁵ Instead, these authors maintain that "African Americans are much more likely than are white candidates to be urged to run by people from their churches, their neighborhoods, and their families."³⁶

On the other hand, Lawless documents that people of color reported higher levels of recruitment: "All else equal, and across political parties and professions, black eligible candidates are more than 14 percentage points more likely than their white or Latino counterparts to report having been recruited to run for office by an electoral gatekeeper."³⁷ Part of the discrepancy is probably attributable to the time frames. Perhaps Lawless is picking up a change in the recruitment patters of political parties over time. Nonetheless, none of these studies offers an analysis of gender. Are women of color recruited by political parties at the same rates as their white female and male of color counterparts? This is still an open question.

FINAL REMARKS

Although women of all colors have come a long way, their service in our legislative institutions is far from equal. A few states come close to parity, but in some states, women make up only 10% of their legislative bodies. Furthermore, this level of representation varies by race/ethnicity. Gender and race continue to organize our political experience in the United States, as our governing institutions do not descriptively mirror the population. If representation is at the heart of democracy, then what does it mean when entire groups of citizens do not have a voice at the political table? Descriptive representation is an important function of democracy in that one's voice is reflected in the debate—if groups are descriptively represented in an institution, then there is at least the potential to exercise political power.[38]

Scholars have already established that this lack of descriptive representation has participatory effects. Women are less engaged politically at the mass level, but this trend is reversed when women are represented by women. So, when women are represented by women they do and know more about politics. The same holds for people of color. Looking at the disparity in political engagement from this angle points to a larger understanding of how underrepresentation affects political participation in general. Perhaps this depressed level of participation would not be as important if women and people of color did not have distinct policy preferences. But, they do. Plus, substantively, women legislators and legislators of color have different political agendas from their gender and racial counterparts when they are present in our legislative institutions, thereby providing substantive representation, at least to a certain degree.

The key idea I would like readers to take away from this project is the importance of intersecting identities. My findings are merely a stepping-stone for future research. Although I have offered a portion of the picture and some speculations as to the possible reasons for the results, the full portrait has yet to be discovered, and this study highlights the need to explore many questions that are still left unanswered. Exactly *how* and *why* gender and race/ethnicity are intersecting is underexplored in terms of legislative office holding. To be sure, the process seems to be more complex that what is captured by race/ethnicity *or* gender separately. Although I have imposed the same (perhaps rigid) model on all women of color for reasons of parsimony, the evidence suggests that this all-encompassing model does not help explain all of the variance we see in state legislative office holding. Dissecting the conventional approaches and rethinking them from an intersectional perspective will allow us to get a better handle on how intersectionality informs descriptive representation. As we move forward, it might be wise to integrate our understandings of gender and race and to ask why, where, when, and how do each of the variables matter, and for whom?

NOTES

1. See Table 5.2 in Chapter 5 for a summary of these predictions.
2. Luis Ricardo Fraga, Valerie Martinez-Ebers, Linda Lopez, and Ricardo Ramirez, "Gender and Ethnicity: Patterns of Electoral Success and Legislative Advocacy among Latina and Latino State Officials in Four States," *Journal of Women, Politics and Policy* 28, no. 3–4 (2006): 122–145.
3. Fraga et al. contend that a "focus on the state level is designed to move beyond understandings based solely on national trends that may mask significant variation across states regarding the political incorporation of communities of color." See Fraga et al., "Gender and Ethnicity: Patterns of Electoral Success," 123.
4. Paule Cruz Takash, "Breaking Barriers to Representation: Chicana/Latina Elected Officials in California" in *Women Transforming Politics: An Alternative Reader*, ed. Cathy J. Cohen, Kathleen B. Jones, and Joan C. Tronto (New York: New York University Press, 1997), 423.
5. Katherine Tate, *Black Faces in the Mirror: African Americans and Their Representatives in the U.S. Congress* (Chicago: University of Chicago Press, 2003), 63, 64.
6. Katherine Tate, *Black Faces in the Mirror*, 64.
7. Albert K. Karing and Susan Welch, "Sex and Ethnic Differences in Municipal Representation," *Social Science Quarterly* 60, no. 3 (December 1979), 479.
8. Nancy Burns, Kay Lehman Schlozman, and Sidney Verba, *The Private Roots of Public Action: Gender, Equality, and Political Participation* (Cambridge, MA: Harvard University Press, 2001).
9. However, when women are represented by a female office holder, those women report higher feelings of political efficacy, higher rates of political participation, and higher recollection of the representative's name. See Burns, Schlozman, and Verba, *The Private Roots of Public Action*.
10. Jennifer Lawless, *Becoming a Candidate: Political Ambition and the Decision to Run for Office* (New York: Cambridge University Press, 2012); Jennifer L. Lawless and Richard L. Fox, *It Takes a Candidate: Why Women Don't Run for Office* (New York: Cambridge University Press, 2005); and Jennifer Lawless and Richard Fox, *It Still Takes a Candidate: Why Women Don't Run for Office* New York: Cambridge University Press, 2010).

11. Katherine Tate, "African American Female Senatorial Candidates: Twin Assets or Double Liabilities?," in *African American Power and Politics: The Political Context Variable*, ed. Hanes Walton Jr. (New York: Columbia University Press, 1997), 63.
12. Robert Darcy and Charles D. Hadley, "Black Women in Politics: The Puzzle of Success," *Social Science Quarterly* 69, no. 3 (September 1988): 642.
13. Gary Moncrief, Joel Thompson, and Robert Schuhmann, "Gender, Race, and the State Legislature: A Research Note on the Double Disadvantage Hypothesis," *Social Science Journal* 28 (1991): 481–487.
14. Lawless and Fox, *It Takes a Candidate*; Lawless and Fox, *It Still Takes a Candidate*; and Lawless, *Becoming a Candidate*, 194.
15. Lawless, *Becoming a Candidate*; Lawless and Fox, *It Takes a Candidate*; and Lawless and Fox, *It Still Takes a Candidate*.
16. Williams, "The Civil Rights-Black Power Legacy: Black Women Elected Officials at the Local, State, and National Levels," in *Sisters in the Struggle: African American Women in the Civil Rights-Black Power Movement*, ed. Bettye Collier-Thomas and V.P. Franklin (New York: New York University Press, 2001), 313.
17. Williams, "The Civil Rights-Black Power Legacy"; Jewel Prestage, "Black Women State Legislators: A Profile," in *A Portrait of Marginality: The Political Behavior of the American Woman*, ed. M. Githens and J.L. Prestage (New York: David McKay, 1977), 400–418; Darcy and Hadley, "Black Women in Politics"; Moncrief, Thompson, and Schuhmann, "Gender, Race, and the State Legislature."
18. Paule Cruz Takash, "Breaking Barriers to Representation: Chicana/Latina Elected Officials in California," in *Women Transforming Politics: An Alternative Reader*, ed. Cathy J. Cohen, Kathleen B. Jones, and Joan C. Tronto (New York: New York University Press, 1997), 412–434.
19. James Button and David Hedge, "Legislative Life in the 1990s: A Comparison of Black and White State Legislators," *Legislative Studies Quarterly* 21, no. 2 (May 1996): 203.
20. Ibid.
21. Kim Geron and James S. Lai, "Beyond Symbolic Representation: A Comparison of the Electoral Pathways and Policy Priorities of Asian American and Latino Elected Officials," *Asian Law Journal* 9 (May 2002): 61. Neither Geron and Lai nor Button and Hedge discuss how their results differ by gender.
22. Jerry Perkins, "Political Ambition among Black and White Women: An Intragender Test of the Socialization Model," *Women & Politics* 6, no. 1 (Spring 1986): 27–40

23. Perkins, "Political Ambition," 36 (italics in original).
24. Sonia R. Garcia and Marisela Marquez, "Motivational and Attitudinal Factors amongst Latinas in U.S. Electoral Politics," *NWSA Journal* 13, no. 2 (Summer 2001): 120.
25. Katherine Tate, *Black Faces in the Mirror*, 63.
26. Williams, "The Civil Rights-Black Power Legacy."
27. Ibid.; Tate, *Black Faces in the Mirror*; Wendy Smooth, "Intersectionality in Electoral Politics: A Mess Worth Making," *Politics & Gender* 2, no. 3 (2006): 400–414; Wendy Smooth, "African American Women and Electoral Politics: A Challenge to the Post-Race Rhetoric of the Obama Movement," in *Gender and Elections: Shaping the Future of American Politics*, ed. Susan J. Carroll and Richard Logan Fox (New York: Cambridge University Press, 2010) 165–86; and Rosalee A. Clawson and John A. Clark, "The Attitudinal Structure of African American Women Party Activists: The Impact of Race, Gender and Religion," *Political Research Quarterly* 56, no. 2 (2003): 211–221.
28. Clawson and Clark, "Attitudinal Structure," 219.
29. Robert Moore, "Religion, Race, and Gender Differences in Political Ambition," *Politics & Gender* 1, no. 4 (2005): 577–596; and Angela Frederick, "Bringing Narrative In: Race-Gender Storytelling, Political Ambition, and Women's Path to Public Office," *Journal of Women, Politics & Policy* 34, no. 2 (2013): 113–137.
30. Moore, "Religion, Race, and Gender Differences," in Political Ambition," 593.
31. Frederick, "Bringing Narrative In," 113.
32. K. Sanbonmatsu, *Where Women Run: Gender and Party in the American States* (Ann Arbor: University of Michigan Press, 2006).
33. Thomas E. Cavanagh and Denise Stockton, *Black Elected Officials and Their Constituencies* (Washington, DC: Joint Center for Political Studies), 1983.
34. Gary F. Moncrief, Peverill Squire, and Malcolm E. Jewell, *Who Runs for the Legislature?* (Upper Saddle River, NJ: Prentice Hall, 2001), 108.
35. Ibid.
36. Ibid.
37. Lawless, *Becoming a Candidate*, 150.
38. Suzanne Dovi, "Preferable Descriptive Representatives: Will Just Any Woman, Black, or Latino Do?" *American Political Science Review* 96, no. 4 (December 2002): 729–743; and Jane Mansbridge, "Should Women Represent Women and Blacks Represent Blacks? A Contingent 'Yes,'" *Journal of Politics* 61, no. 3 (August 1999): 628–657.

References

Arceneaux, Kevin. "The 'Gender Gap' in State Legislative Representation: New Data to Tackle and Old Question." *Political Research Quarterly* 54 (2001): 143–160.

Barrett Edith J. "The Policy Priorities of African-American Women in State Legislatures." *Legislative Studies Quarterly* 20, no. 2 (May 1995): 223–247.

Barrett, Edith J. "Black Women in State Legislatures: The Relationship of Race and Gender to the Legislative Experience." In *The Impact of Women in Public Office*, edited by Susan J. Carroll, 185–204. Bloomington: Indiana University Press, 2001.

Barrett, Edith J. "Gender and Race in the State House: The Legislative Experience." *The Social Science Journal* 34, no. 2 (1997): 105–269.

Barreto, Matt A. "¡Sí Se Puede! Latino Candidates and the Mobilization of Latino Voters." *American Political Science Review* 101, no. 3 (August 2007): 425–441.

Baxter, Sandra, and Marjorie Lansing. *Women and Politics: The Visible Majority*. Ann Arbor: University of Michigan Press, 1983.

Bobo, Lawrence, and Franklin D. Gilliam. "Race, Sociopolitical Participation, and Black Empowerment." *American Political Science Review* 84 (1990): 377–393.

Bratton, Kathleen A. "The Behavior and Success of Latino Legislators: Evidence from the States." *Social Science Quarterly* 87, no. 5 (December 2006): 1136–1157.

Bratton, Kathleen A., and Kerry L. Haynie. "Agenda Setting and Legislative Success in State Legislatures: The Effects of Gender and Race." *The Journal of Politics* 61, no. 3 (1999): 658–679.

Bratton, Kathleen A., Kerry L. Haynie, and Beth Reingold. "Agenda Setting and African American Women in State Legislatures." Paper presented at the Annual Meeting of the American Political Science Association, Washington, DC, Sept. 1–4, 2005.

Brians, Craig Leonard. "Women for Women? Gender and Party Bias in Voting for Female Candidates." *American Politics Research* 33, no. 3 (May 2005): 357–375.

Browning, Rufus P., Dale Rogers Marshall, David H. Tabb: *Racial Politics in American Cities.* 3rd ed. Upper Saddle River, NJ: Pearson, 2002.

Bryce, Herrington J., and Alan E. Warrick. "Black Women in Electoral Politics." In *A Portrait of Marginality: The Political Behavior of the American Woman*, edited by M. Githens and J. L. Prestage, 395–400. New York: David McKay, 1977.

Bullock, Charles S. "The Election of Blacks in the South: Preconditions and Consequences." *American Journal of Political Science* 19, no. 4 (November 1975): 727–739.

Burns, Nancy, Kay Lehman Schlozman, and Sidney Verba. *The Private Roots of Public Action: Gender, Equality, and Political Participation.* Cambridge, MA: Harvard University Press, 2001.

Burrell, Barbara. *A Woman's Place Is in the House: Campaigning for Congress in the Feminist Era.* Ann Arbor: University of Michigan Press, 1994.

Burrell, Barbara. "Campaign Finance: Women's Experience in the Modern Era." In *Women in Elected Office: Past, Present, and Future*, edited by Sue Thomas and Clyde Wilcox, 26–37. New York, NY: Oxford University Press, 1998.

Burrell, Barbara. "Women Candidates in Open Seat Primaries for the U.S. House of Representatives, 1968–1990." *Legislative Studies Quarterly* 17, no. 4 (November 1992): 493–508.

Burrell, Barbara. "Women's and Men's Campaigns for the U.S. House of Representatives, 1972–1982: A Finance Gap?" *American Politics Quarterly* (July 1985): 251–272.

Button, James, and David Hedge. "Legislative Life in the 1990s: A Comparison of Black and White State Legislators." *Legislative Studies Quarterly* 21, no. 2 (May 1996): 199–218.

Camobreco, John F., and Michelle A. Barnello. "Postmaterialism and Post-Industrialism: Cultural Influences on Female Representation in State Legislatures." *State Politics and Policy Quarterly* 3, no. 2 (Summer 2003): 117–138.

Canon, David T. *Race, Redistricting, and Representation: The Unintended Consequences of Black Majority Districts.* Chicago: University of Chicago Press, 1999.

Caress, Stanley. "The Influence of Term Limits on the Electoral Success of Women." *Women and Politics* 20, no. 3 (1999): 45–63.

Carroll, Susan J. "Representing Women: Women State Legislators as Agents of Policy-Related Change." In *The Impact of Women in Public Office*, edited by Susan J. Carroll, 3–21. Bloomington: Indiana University Press, 2001.

Carroll, Susan J. *Women as Candidates in American Politics.* 2nd ed. Bloomington, IN: Indiana University Press, 1994.

Carroll, Susan J., and Krista Jenkins. "Do Term Limits Help Women Get Elected?" *Social Science Quarterly* 82, no. 1 (March 2001): 197–201.

Carroll, Susan J., and Krista Jenkins. "Increasing Diversity or More of the Same? Term Limits and the Representation of Women, Minorities, and Minority Women in State Legislatures." Paper presented at the American Political Science Association's annual meeting, San Francisco, August 30–September 2, 2001.

Carroll, Susan J., and Krista Jenkins. "Unrealized Opportunity? Term Limits and the Representation of Women in State Legislatures." *Women and Politics* 23, no. 4 (2001): 1–30.

Casellas, Jason P. *Latino Representation in State Houses and Congress.* Cambridge: Cambridge University Press, 2011.

Casellas, Jason P. "The Institutional and Demographic Determinants of Latino Representation." *Legislative Studies Quarterly* 34, no. 3 (August 2009): 399–425.

Cavanagh, Thomas E., and Denise Stockton. *Black Elected Officials and their Constituencies.* Washington, DC: Joint Center for Political Studies, 1983.

Ceaser, James W., and Robert P. Saldin. "A New Measure of Party Strength." *Political Research Quarterly* 58, no. 2 (June 2005): 245–256.

Center for American Women and Politics. "Women of Color in State Legislatures 1990, 1995, 2000, 2005, and 2010." New Brunswick: Eagleton Institute for Politics, Rutgers, State University of New Jersey, November 2010. Personal request.

Center for American Women and Politics. "Women in State Legislatures 2010." New Brunswick: Eagleton Institute for Politics, Rutgers, State University of New Jersey, 2010. http://www.cawp.rutgers.edu/fast_facts/levels_of_office/documents/stleg.pdf.

Center for American Women and Politics. "Women of Color in Elective Office 2010." New Brunswick: Eagleton Institute for Politics, Rutgers, State University of New Jersey, 2010. http://www.cawp.rutgers.edu/fast_facts/levels_of_office/documents/color.pdf.

Clawson, Rosalee. A. and John A. Clark. "The Attitudinal Structure of African American Women Party Activists: The Impact of Race, Gender and Religion." *Political Research Quarterly* 56, no. 2 (2003): 211–21.

Clucas, Richard A. "Improving the Harvest of State Legislative Research." *State Politics and Policy Quarterly* 3, no. 4 (Winter 2003): 387–419.

Cohen, Cathy J. "A Portrait of Marginality: The Study of Women of Color in American Politics." In *Women and American Politics: New Questions, New Directions*, edited by Susan J. Carroll, 190–213. Oxford: Oxford University Press, 2003.

Collins, Todd and Laura Moyer. "Gender, Race, and Intersectionality on the Federal Appellate Bench." *Political Research Quarterly* 61, no. 2 (June 2008): 219–227.

Crenshaw, Kimberle. "Demarginalizing the Intersection of Race and Sex: A Black Feminist Critique of Antidiscrimination Doctrine,

Feminist Theory and Antiracist Politics." *University of Chicago Legal Forum* (1989): 139–167.
Crenshaw, Kimberle. "Mapping the Margins: Intersectionality, Identity Politics, and Violence Against Women of Color." *Stanford Law Review* 43, no. 6 (July 1991): 1241–1299.
Darcy, Robert, and Charles D. Hadley. "Black Women in Politics: The Puzzle of Success." *Social Science Quarterly* 69, no. 3 (Sept. 1988): 629–645.
Darcy, Robert, Charles D. Hadley, and Jason F. Kirksey. "Election Systems and the Representation of Black Women in American State Legislatures." *Women and Politics* 13, no. 2 (1993): 73–89.
Darcy, Robert, Susan Welch, and Janet Clark. *Women, Elections, and Representation*. 2nd ed. Lincoln: Nebraska University Press, 1994.
Darling, Marsha J. "African-American Women in State Elective Office in the South." In *Women and Elective Office: Past, Present and Future*, edited by Sue Thomas and Clyde Wilcox, 150–162. New York: New York University Press, 1998.
Dodson, Debra L. ed. *Gender and Policymaking: Studies of Women in Office*. New Brunswick: Center for American Women and Politics, Eagleton Institute of Politics, Rutgers, the State University of New Jersey, 1991.
Dovi, Suzanne. "Preferable Descriptive Representatives: Will Just Any Woman, Black, or Latino Do?" *American Political Science Review* 96, no. 4 (December 2002): 729–743.
Eisele, Stephen. "Women of Color in American Politics." 2012. Available from the Hunt Alternative's Political Parity Project. http://www.politicalparity.org/.
Elazar, Daniel J. *American Federalism: A View from the States*. New York: Thomas Y. Crowell Company, 1966.
Elazar, Daniel J. *American Federalism: A View from the States*. 3rd ed. New York: Harper Collins College Division, 1984.
Elder, Laura. "The Partisan Gap among Women State Legislators." *Journal of Women, Politics and Policy* 33, no. 1 (2012): 65–85.
Endersby, James W., and Charles E. Menifield. "Representation, Ethnicity, and Congress: Black and Hispanic Representatives and Constituencies." In *Black and Multiracial Politics in America*, edited by Yvette M. Alex-Assensoh and Lawrence J. Hanks, 257–272. New York: New York University Press, 2000.
Erikson, Robert S., Gerald C. Wright, and John P. McIver. "Replication Data for: Public Opinion in the States: A Quarter Century of Change and Stability." 2007. http://hdl.handle.net/1902.1/10442 UNF:3:42A1SVhk3cWA2Ss5az8zjQ.
Fenno, Richard. *Going Home: Black Representatives and their Constituents*. Chicago: University of Chicago Press, 2003.
Fitzpatrick, Jody L., and Rodney E. Hero. "Political Culture and Political Characteristics of the American States: A Consideration

of Some Old and New Questions." *Western Political Quarterly* 41, no. 1 (March 1988): 145–153.
Ford, Lynne E., and Kathleen Dolan. "Women State Legislators: Three Decades of Gains in Representation and Diversity." In *Women and Politics: Outsiders or Insiders? A Collection of Readings*, edited by Lois Lovelace Duke, 203–218. Upper Saddle River, NJ: Prentice Hall, 1999.
Fox, Richard. *Gender Dynamics in Congressional Elections*. Thousand Oaks, CA: Sage, 1997.
Fraga, Luis Ricardo, Linda Lopez, Valerie Martinez-Ebers, and Ricardo Ramirez. "Gender and Ethnicity: Patterns of Electoral Success and Legislative Advocacy among Latina and Latino State Officials in Four States." *Journal of Women, Politics and Policy* 28, no. 3–4 (2006): 122–145.
Fraga, Luis Ricardo, Valerie Martinez-Ebers, Ricardo Ramirez, and Linda Lopez. "Gender and Ethnicity: The Political Incorporation of Latina and Latino State Legislators." Inequality and Social Policy Seminar, John F. Kennedy School of Government, Cambridge, MA, November 10, 2003.
Frederick, Angela. "Bringing Narrative In: Race-Gender Storytelling, Political Ambition, and Women's Path to Public Office." *Journal of Women, Politics & Policy* 34, no. 2 (2013): 113–137.
Galligan, Yvonne, Sara Clavero, and Marina Calloni. *Gender Politics and Democracy in Post-Socialist Europe*. Farmington Hills, MI: Barbara Budrich Publishers, 2007.
Gamble, Katrina L. "Black Political Representation: An Examination of Legislative Activity within U.S. House Committees." *Legislative Studies Quarterly* 32, no. 3 (August 2007): 421–447.
Garcia, Sonia R., and Marisela Marquez. "Motivational and Attitudinal Factors Amongst Latinas in U.S. Electoral Politics." *NWSA Journal* 13, no. 2 (Summer 2001): 112–122.
Gay, Claudine. "The Effect of Black Congressional Representation on Political Participation." *American Political Science Review* 95, no. 3 (2001): 589–602.
Gay, Claudine, and Katherine Tate. "Doubly Bound: The Impact of Gender and Race on the Politics of Black Women." *Political Psychology* 19, no. 1 (1998): 169–184.
Gerber, Elisabeth R., Rebecca B. Morton, and Thomas A. Rietz. "Minority Representation in Multimember Districts." *American Political Science Review* 92, no. 1 (March 1998): 127–144.
Geron, Kim, and James S. Lai. "Beyond Symbolic Representation: A Comparison of the Electoral Pathways and Policy Priorities of Asian American and Latino Elected Officials." *Asian Law Journal* 9 (May 2002): 41–81.
Githens, Marianne, and Jewel L. Prestage. *A Portrait of Marginality: The Political Behavior of the American Woman*. New York: David McKay Company, Inc., 1977.

Grofman, Bernard, and Lisa Handley. "Black Representation: Making Sense of Electoral Geography at Different Levels of Government." *Legislative Studies Quarterly* 14, no. 2 (May 1989): 265–279.

Grofman, Bernard, and Lisa Handley. "Minority Population Proportion and Black and Hispanic Congressional Success in the 1970s and 1980s." *American Politics Quarterly* 17, no. 4 (October 1989): 436–445.

Grofman, Bernard, and Lisa Handley. "The Impact of the Voting Rights Act on Black Representation in Southern State Legislatures." *Legislative Studies Quarterly* 16, no. 1 (February 1991): 111–128.

Grose, Christian R. *Congress in Black and White: Race and Representation in Washington and at Home.* New York: Cambridge University Press, 2011.

Haney López, Ian. *White by Law: The Legal Construction of Race.* New York: New York University Press, 2006.

Hardy-Fanta, Carol. *Latina Politics, Latino Politics: Gender, Culture, and Political Participation in Boston.* Philadelphia: Temple University Press, 1993.

Hardy-Fanta, Carol, Pei-te Lien, Christine Marie Sierra, and Dianne M. Pinderhughes. "A New Look at Paths to Political Office: Moving Women of Color from the Margins to the Center." Paper presented at the Annual Meeting of the American Political Science Association, Chicago, August 30–September 2, 2007.

Hardy-Fanta, Carol, Christine M. Sierra, Pei-te Lien, Dianne M. Pinderhughes, and Wartnya L. Davis. "Race, Gender, and Descriptive Representation in the US: An Exploratory View of Multicultural Elected Leadership in the United States." Paper presented at the annual meeting of the American Political Science Association, Washington, DC, September 1, 2005.

Hardy-Fanta, Carol, Pei-te Lien, Dianne M. Pinderhughes, and Christine Marie Sierra. "Gender, Race, and Descriptive Representation in the United States: Findings from the Gender and Multicultural Leadership Project." *Journal of Women, Politics and Policy* 28, no. 3–4 (2006): 7–41.

Hawkesworth, Mary. "Congressional Enactments of Race-Gender: Toward a Theory of Raced-Gendered Institutions." *American Political Science Review* 97, no. 4 (November 2003): 529–550.

Haynie, Kerry. *African American State Legislators in the American States.* New York: Columbia University Press, 2001.

Hedge, David, James Button, and Mary Spear. "Accounting for the Quality of Black Legislative Life: The View from the States." *American Journal of Political Science* 40, no. 1 (1996): 82–98.

Hero, Rodney E. *Faces of Inequality: Social Diversity in American Politics.* New York: Oxford University Press, 1998.

Hero, Rodney E., and Caroline J. Tolbert. "Racial/Ethnic Diversity Interpretation of Politics and Policy in the States of the U.S."

American Journal of Political Science 40, no. 3 (August 1996): 851–871.

Hill, David B. "Political Culture and Female Political Representation." *The Journal of Politics* 43 (1981): 159–168.

Hogan, Robert E. "The Influences of State and District Conditions on the Representation of Women in U.S. State Legislatures." *American Politics Research* 29 (2001): 4–24.

Jewell, Malcom E. *Representation in State Legislatures*. Lexington: University of Kentucky Press, 1982.

Johnson, Charles A. "Political Culture in American States: Elazar's Formulation Examined." *American Journal of Political Science* 20, no. 3 (August 1976): 491–509.

Junn, Jane. "Assimilating or Coloring Participation? Gender, Race, and Democratic Political Participation." In *Women Transforming Politics: An Alternative Reader*, edited by Cathy J. Cohen, Kathleen B. Jones, and Joan C. Tronto, 387–397. New York: New York University Press, 1997.

Karing, Albert K. and Susan Welch. "Sex and Ethnic Differences in Municipal Representation." *Social Science Quarterly* 60, no. 3 (December 1979): 465–480.

King, James D. "Single-Member Districts and the Representation of Women in American State Legislatures: The Effects of Electoral System Change." *State Politics and Policy Quarterly* 2, no. 2 (Summer 2002): 161–175.

Kittilson, Miki Caul. *Challenging Parties, Changing Parliaments: Women and Elected Office in Contemporary Western Europe*. Columbus, OH: Ohio State University Press, 2006.

Lai, James S., Wendy K. Tam Cho, Thomas P. Kim, and Okiyoshi Takeda. "Asian Pacific-American Campaigns, Elections, and Elected Officials." *PS: Political Science and Politics* 34, no. 3 (Sept. 2001): 611–617.

Lawless, Jennifer. *Becoming a Candidate: Political Ambition and the Decision to Run for Office*. New York: Cambridge University Press, 2012.

Lawless, Jennifer L., and Richard L. Fox. *It Takes a Candidate: Why Women Don't Run for Office*. New York: Cambridge University Press, 2005.

Lawless, Jennifer, and Richard Fox. *It Still Takes a Candidate: Why Women Don't Run for Office*. New York: Cambridge University Press, 2010.

Lien, Pei-te, Carol Hardy-Fanta, Dianne M. Pinderhughes, and Christine Marie Sierra. "Expanding Categorization at the Intersection of Race and Gender: 'Women of Color' as a Political Category for African American, Latina, Asian American, and American Indian Women." Paper presented at the Annual Meeting of the American Political Science Association, Boston, August 27–31, 2008.

Lien, Pei-te, Dianne M. Pinderhughes, Carol Hardy-Fanta, and Christine Marie Sierra. "The Voting Rights Act and the Election of Nonwhite Officials." *PS: Political Science & Politics* 40, no. 3 (2007): 489–94.

Lublin, David. *The Paradox of Representation: Racial Gerrymandering and Minority Interests in Congress.* Princeton, NJ: Princeton University Press, 1997.

Mansbridge, Jane. "Should Blacks Represent Blacks and Women Represent Women? A Contingent 'Yes.'" *Journal of Politics* 61, no. 3 (August 1999): 628–657.

Mansbridge, Jane, and Katherine Tate. "Race Trumps Gender: The Thomas Nomination in the Black Community." *PS: Political Science & Politics* 25, no. 3 (1992): 488–92.

Matland, Richard E., and Deborah Dwight Brown. "District Magnitude's Effect on Female Representation in U.S. State Legislatures." *Legislative Studies Quarterly* 17, no. 4 (November 1992): 469–492.

Matson, Marsha, and Terri Susan Fine. "Gender, Ethnicity, and Ballot Information: Ballot Cues in Low-Information Elections." *State Politics and Policy Quarterly* 6, no. 1 (Spring 2006): 49–72.

Minta, Michael D. *Oversight: Representing the Interest of Blacks and Latinos in Congress.* Princeton, NJ: Princeton University Press, 2011.

Moncrief, Gary F., and Joel A. Thompson. "Electoral Structures and State Legislative Representation: A Research Note." *Journal of Politics* 54, no. 1 (February 1992): 246–256.

Moncrief, Gary, Joel Thompson, and Robert Schuhmann. "Gender, Race, and the State Legislature: A Research Note on the Double Disadvantage Hypothesis." *Social Science Journal* 28 (1991): 481–87.

Moncrief, Gary F., Peverill Squire, and Malcolm E. Jewell. *Who Runs for the Legislature?* Upper Saddle River, NJ: Prentice Hall, 2001.

Montoya, Lisa J., Carol Hardy-Fanta, and Sonia Garcia. "Latina Politics: Gender, Participation, and Leadership." *PS: Political Science and Politics* 33, no. 3 (September 2000): 555–561.

Mooney, Christopher Z. "State Politics and Policy Quarterly and the Study of State Politics: The Editor's Introduction." *State Politics and Policy Quarterly* (Spring 2001): 1–4.

Moore, Robert. "Religion, Race, and Gender Differences in Political Ambition." *Politics & Gender* 1, no. 4 (2005): 577–596.

Nechemias, Carol. "Changes in the Election of Women to U.S. State Legislative Seats." *Legislative Studies Quarterly*, 8, no. 1 (1987): 125–142.

Nelson, Albert. *Emerging Influentials in State Legislatures: Women, Blacks, and Hispanics.* Westport, CT: Praeger, 1991.

Niven, David. *The Missing Majority: The Recruitment of Women as State Legislative Candidates.* Westport, CT: Praeger, 1998.

Norrander, Barbara, and Clyde Wilcox. "Change in Continuity in the Geography of Women State Legislators." In *Women and Elective Office: Past, Present, and Future*, 2nd ed., edited by Sue Thomas and Clyde Wilcox, 176–196. New York: Oxford University Press, 2005.

Norrander, Barbara, and Clyde Wilcox. "Change in Continuity in the Geography of Women State Legislators." In *Women and Elective Office: Past, Present, and Future*, 2nd ed., edited by Sue Thomas and Clyde Wilcox, 176–196. New York: Oxford University Press, 2005.

Norrander, Barbara, and Clyde Wilcox. "The Geography of Gender Power: Women in State Legislatures." In *Women and Elective Office: Past, Present, and Future*, edited by Sue Thomas and Clyde Wilcox, 103–117. New York: Oxford University Press, 1998.

Orey, Byron D., and Wendy Smooth, with Kimberly S. Adams and Kisha H. Clark. "Race and Gender Matter: Refining Models of Legislative Policy Making in State Legislatures." *Journal of Women, Politics & Policy* 28, no. 314 (2006): 97–119.

Ostrander, Katie E., and Pei-te Lien. "Structural and Contextual Factors in the Election of Women and Minorities to Sub-National Offices: A Review of the Literature." Paper presented at the Annual Meeting of the Western Political Science Association, San Francisco, April 1–3, 2010.

Owens, Chris T. "Black Substantive Representation in State Legislatures from 1971–1994." *Social Science Quarterly* 86, no. 4 (December 2005): 779–791.

Oxley, Zoe M., and Richard L. Fox. "Women in Executive Office: Variation across American States." *Political Research Quarterly* 57, no. 1 (March 2004): 113–120.

Pachon, Harry, and Louis DeSipio. "Latino Elected Officials in the 1990s." *PS: Political Science and Politics* 25, no. 2 (June 1992): 212–217.

Palmer, Barbara, and Dennis Simon. *Breaking the Political Glass Ceiling: Women and Congressional Elections*. 2nd ed. New York: Routledge, 2008.

Palmer, Barbara, and Dennis Simon. *Women and Congressional Elections: A Century of Change*. Boulder, CO: Lynne Rienner Publishers, 2012.

Pardo, Mary S. *Mexican American Women Activists: Identity and Resistance in Two Los Angeles Communities*. Philadelphia: Temple University Press, 1998.

Pateman, Carol. *The Disorder of Women: Democracy, Feminism, and Political Theory*. Stanford, CA: Stanford University Press, 1989.

Perkins, Jerry. "Political Ambition among Black and White Women: An Intragender Test of the Socialization Model." *Women & Politics* 6, no. 1 (Spring 1986): 27–40.

Philpot, Tasha S., and Hanes Walton, Jr. "One of Our Own: Black Female Candidates and the Voters Who Support Them." *American Journal of Political Science* 51, no. 1 (2007): 49–62.

Prestage, Jewel. "Black Women State Legislators: A Profile." In *A Portrait of Marginality: The Political Behavior of the American Woman*, edited by M. Githens and J. L. Prestage, 400–418. New York: David McKay, 1977.

Prestage, Jewel L. "In Quest of African American Political Woman." *Annals of the American Academy of Political and Social Science* 515 (May 1991): 88–103.

Prindeville, Diane. "Feminist Nations? A Study of Native American Women in Southwestern Tribal Politics." *Political Research Quarterly* 57, no. 1 (2004): 101–112.

Prindeville, Diane-Michele, and Teresa Braley Gomez. "American Indian Women Leaders, Public Policy, and the Importance of Gender and Ethnic Identity." *Women and Politics* 20, no. 2 (1991): 17–32.

Pritchard, Anita. "Changes in Electoral Structures and the Success of Women Candidates: The Case of Florida." *Social Science Quarterly* 73, no. 1 (1992): 62–70.

Rule, Wilma. "Multimember Legislative Districts: Minority and Anglo Women's and Men's Recruitment Opportunity." In *United States Electoral Systems: Their Impact on Women and Minorities*, edited by Wilma Rule and Joseph F. Zimmerman, 57–72. Westport, CT: Praeger, 1992.

Rule, Wilma. "Why Are More Women State Legislators?" In *Women in Politics: Outsiders or Insiders?*, 3rd ed., edited by Lois Duke Whitaker, 190–201. Upper Saddle River, NJ: Prentice Hall, 1999.

Rule, Wilma. "Why More Women Are State Legislators: A Research Note." *Western Political Quarterly* 43, no. 2 (1990): 432–448.

Rule, Wilma and Pippa Norris. "Anglo and Minority Women's Underrepresentation in Congress: Is the Electoral System the Culprit?" In *United States Electoral Systems: Their Impact on Women and Minorities*, edited by Wilma Rule and Joseph F. Zimmerman, 41–54. New York: Greenwood Press, 1992.

Saint-Germain, Michelle. "Patterns of Legislative Opportunity in Arizona: Sex, Race, and Ethnicity." In *The Impact of U.S. Electoral Systems on Minorities and Women*, edited by W. Rule and J. F. Zimmerman, 119–128. Westport, CT: Greenwood Press, 1992.

Sanbonmatsu, K. "Political Parties and the Recruitment of Women to State Legislatures." *Journal of Politics* 64, no. 3 (August 2002): 791–809.

Sanbonmatsu, Kira. *Where Women Run: Gender and Party in the American States*. Ann Arbor: University of Michigan Press, 2006.

Sapiro, Virginia. "When Are Interests Interesting? The Problem of Political Representation of Women." *American Political Science Review* 75 (September 1981): 701–16. Reprinted in Anne Phillips, ed., *Feminism and Politics*, 161–92. New York: Oxford University Press, 1998.

Schaffner, Brian F. "Priming Gender: Campaigning on Women's Issues in U.S. Senate Elections." *American Journal of Political Science* 49, no. 4 (October 2005): 803–817.

Scola, Becki. "Predicting Presence at the Intersections: Assessing the Variation in Women's Office Holding across the States," *State Politics & Policy Quarterly* 13, no. 3 (2013): 333–348.
Scola, Becki. "Women of Color in State Legislatures: Gender, Race, and Legislative Office Holding." *Journal of Women, Politics, and Policy* 28, no. 3–4 (2006): 43–70.
Segura, Gary M., and Shaun Bowler. *Diversity in Democracy: Minority Representation in the United States*. Charlottesville, VA: University of Virginia Press, 2005.
Sharkansky, Ira. "The Utility of Elazar's Political Culture: A Research Note." *Polity* 2 (1969): 66–83.
Simien, Evelyn. *Black Feminist Voices in Politics*. Albany: State University of New York Press, 2006.
Smith, Rogers. *Civic Ideals: Conflicting Visions of Citizenship in U.S. History*. New Haven, CT: Yale University Press, 1997.
Smooth, Wendy. "African American Women and Electoral Politics: A Challenge to the Post-Race Rhetoric of the Obama Movement." In *Gender and Elections: Shaping the Future of American Politics*, edited by Susan J. Carroll and Richard Logan Fox, 165–86. New York: Cambridge University Press, 2010.
Smooth, Wendy. "African American Women State Legislators: The Impact of Gender and Race on Legislative Influence." Doctoral dissertation, University of Maryland College Park, 2001.
Smooth, Wendy. "Intersectionality in Electoral Politics: A Mess Worth Making." *Politics & Gender* 2, no. 3 (2006): 400–414.
Squire, Peverill. "Legislative Professionalization and Membership Diversity in State Legislatures." *Legislative Studies Quarterly* 17, no. 1 (February 1992): 69–79.
Squire, Peverill. "Measuring State Legislative Professionalism: The Squire Index Revisited." *State Politics and Policy Quarterly* 7, no. 2 (Summer 2007): 211–227.
Stout, Christopher, and Katherine Tate. "The 2008 Presidential Election, Political Efficacy, and Group Empowerment." *Politics, Groups, and Identities* 1, no. 2 (2013): 143–163.
Swain, Carol M. *Black Faces, Black Interests: The Representation of African Americans in Congress*. Cambridge, MA: Harvard University Press, 1995.
Swers, Michele L. *The Difference Women Make: The Policy Impact of Women on Congress*. Chicago: University of Chicago Press, 2002.
Takash, Paule Cruz. "Breaking Barriers to Representation: Chicana/Latina Elected Officials in California." In *Women Transforming Politics: An Alternative Reader*, edited by Cathy J. Cohen, Kathleen B. Jones, and Joan C. Tronto, 412–434. New York: New York University Press, 1997.
Tate, Katherine. "African American Female Senatorial Candidates: Twin Assets or Double Liabilities?" In *African American Power and Politics: The Political Context Variable*, edited by Hanes

Walton, Jr., 264–281. New York: Columbia University Press, 1997.

Tate, Katherine. *Black Faces in the Mirror: African Americans and Their Representatives in the U.S. Congress*. Chicago: University of Chicago Press, 2003.

Thomas, Sue. "The Impact of Women on State Legislative Policies." *Journal of Politics* 53, no. 4 (1991): 958–76.

Thomas, Sue. "Women in State Legislatures: One Step at a Time." In *The Year of the Woman: Myths and Realities*, edited by Elizabeth Adell Cook, Sue Thomas, and Clyde Wilcox, 148–155. San Francisco: Westview Press, 1994.

Thomas, Sue, and Susan Welch. "The Impact of Women in State Legislatures: Numerical and Organizational Strength." In *The Impact of Women in Public Office*, edited by Susan J. Carroll, 166–181. Bloomington: Indiana University Press, 2001.

Trounstine, Jessica. "All Politics is Local: The Reemergence of the Study of City Politics." *Perspectives on Politics* 7, no. 3 (September 2009): 611–618.

Uhlaner, Carole Jean, and Kay Lehman Schlozman. "Candidate Gender and Congressional Campaign Receipts." *Journal of Politics* 48, no. 1 (1986): 30–50

Uhlaner, Carole, Katie Cooper, and Becki Scola. *The Effect of Descriptive Representation on Participation: Race, Ethnicity, Gender and Voter Turnout across the States*. 2013. Unpublished Manuscript.

United States Census Bureau. "United States Census 1990, Summary File 3." 1990. http://factfinder.census.gov/servlet/DatasetMainPageServlet?_ds_name=DEC_1990_STF3_&_program=DEC&_lang=en.

United States Census Bureau. "United States Census 2000, Summary File 3." 2000. http://www.census.gov/Press-Release/www/2002/sumfile3.html.

United States Census Bureau. "United States Census 2010, Summary File 2." 2010. http://www.census.gov/2010census/data/.

Verba, Sidney, Nancy Burns, Kay Lehman Schlozman. "Knowing and Caring about Politics: Gender and Political Engagement." *Journal of Politics* 59, no. 4 (November 1997): 1051–1072.

Verba, Sidney, Kay Lehman Schlozman, and Henry Brady. *Voice and Equality: Civic Voluntarism in American Politics*. Cambridge, MA: Harvard University Press, 1995.

Welch, Susan, and John R. Hibbing. "Hispanic Representation in the U.S. Congress." *Social Science Quarterly* 65, no. 2 (June 1984): 328–335.

Welch, Susan, and Rebekah Herrick. "The Impact of At-Large Elections on the Representation of Minority Women." In *United States Electoral Systems: Their Impact on Women and Minorities*, edited by Wilma Rule and Joseph F. Zimmerman, 153–166. New York: Greenwood Press, 1992.

Whitby, Kenny J. *The Color of Representation: Congressional Behavior and Black Interests*. Ann Arbor: University of Michigan Press, 1997.

Williams, Linda Faye. "The Civil Rights-Black Power Legacy: Black Women Elected Officials at the Local, State, and National Levels." In *Sisters in the Struggle: African American Women in the Civil Rights-Black Power Movement*, edited by Bettye Collier-Thomas and V. P. Franklin, 306–331. New York: New York University Press, 2001.

Wilson, Walter Clark. "Latino Congressional Staffers and Policy Responsiveness: An Analysis of Latino Interest Agenda Setting." *Politics, Groups, and Identities* 1, no. 2 (2013): 164–180.

Index

African American men *see* black men; men of color
African American women *see* black women; women of color
aggregative process 19n12
ambition, in women 25, 117–20
American Indians *see* Native American men; Native American women
Anglo men *see* white men
Anglo women *see* white women
Asian American legislators 10; data on 56, 57, 118
Asian American men: percentage of in legislatures 86; *see also* Asian American legislators; men of color
Asian American women: as legislators 114; percentage of in legislatures 10; *see also* Asian American legislators; women of color

black electorate 15, 34
black legislators 10, 56, 57, 86
black men: districts of 30, 35; election of 30, 31; at local level 49–50n49; in politics 118, 120; in single-member districts 41; *see also* black electorate; black legislators; men of color
black women: ambition of 32, 117–20; data on 56, 114; districts of 30, 35; election of 31, 115; identities of 29; as legislators 10–11, 54; in multimember districts 41, 116; and politics 117–19, 120; *see also* black electorate; black legislators; women of color

candidates: pool of 36, 37, 87, 116–17; recruitment of 90, 120; women in potential pool of 27–8
Center for American Women and Politics (CAWP) 56, 57, 58
civil rights 117, 118
Congress: race and gender in 30; women in 1
congressional districts: characteristics of 3; elections in 26; *see also* multimember districts; single-member districts; "women-friendly" districts
conservative political ideology 27, 38, 88, 92, 119
cultures *see* political cultures

data, collection of 56–8, 83n5, 86–7, 99n1
deliberative process 19n12
Democratic Party 2, 27, 30, 32, 88, 100–101n16, 117
districts: *see* multimember districts; single-member

districts; "women-friendly" districts
double-disadvantage hypothesis 10, 14, 32
double jeopardy, at local level 49–50n49

Elazar's categories (of variables) 87–8, 102n25
elections: black voting rate in 20n13; of minorities 7, 34; women candidates in 5, 58
electoral structures 34
ethnicity: analysis of 3; and gender 86; as voting cue 5; *see also* race/ethnicity

fund-raising 1

gender: influence of 16, 17; and political participation 20n13; and race/ethnicity 3, 29, 30, 33–4, 103, 110, 113, 115, 121; as voting cue 5; *see also* gender gap
gender gap: assessing 1–2, 4, 37, 55–6; data for 104; factors influencing 24; increase/decrease in 74–6, 79–81, 84n18; in legislators of color 16–17, 25, 73–6, 82, 103–7, 112, 113, 114, 115; racial/ethnic 106, 113; states with highest 77; states with highest decreases in 80; states with highest increases in 79; states with lowest 78; white 16, 25, 73–6, 105, 107, 112–14; and women of color 10, 14, 16, 72–3
geographical variation 11, 13–14, 15–16, 23n35, 25–6, 34, 35, 44n5, 55, 58–64, 86–7, 96, 103, 112

Hispanic men *see* Latinos
Hispanic women *see* Latinas

Independent scales 87
intersectionality: theory of, 14, 29–31, 36, 112; typology of 41–2

Jim Crow South 15
Johnson's scale 87
judiciary, impact of race and gender on 29

Latinas: election of 30, 31, 115; and the gender gap 106; growth in representation by 33; in politics 119; professions of 118; as representatives 10, 56, 57, 84n17, 114; *see also* legislators of color; women of color
Latinos: election of 31; growth in representation by 33; in legislatures 10, 34, 35, 56, 57, 84n17, 86, 102n24; office holding by 38, 95; in politics 118; representation of 34; in single-member districts 41; voting by 115; *see also* legislators of color; men of color
legislation, state level 21n22
legislative professionalization 27, 28–30, 32, 36, 39–40, 89, 95, 98, 104, 105, 106, 107–10, 113
legislative salary, effect of 27, 28–9
legislators of color: analysis of 33–5, 101n20; in Congress 33; data on 57, 112; defined 22n26; gender gap in 103; historical trends for 68–72; increase in women in 110; party affiliation of 88, 100–101n16; percentage of in legislatures 22n29, 86; political agendas of 121;

see also men of color; women of color
liberal political ideology 27, 28, 34, 36, 38–9, 89, 95, 96, 98, 104, 105, 106, 108–9

majority-minority districts 15, 30, 34, 40
majority-party status 32
men, and politics 29, 117
men of color: analysis of 94, 101n20; as candidates 35; compared to women of color 64, 71–2, 103, 110; data on 57, 112; defined 22n26; historical trends for 68–72; percentage of in legislatures 22n29, 86, 95, 111n5; as representatives 32; in single-member districts 107, 116; *see also* men, and politics
minorities: election of 31, 108; in politics 4, 5; representation of 34; as representatives 6
minority population, percentage of 16–17, 27, 28, 34–5, 36, 39, 57, 61, 64, 83n6, 83n15, 88, 89, 92, 95, 98, 103, 104, 105, 106, 108–9, 114
multimember districts (MMDs) 16, 27, 40–41, 89, 90–95, 98, 100n12, 104–7, 109–10, 113, 114–15, 116

National Asian Pacific American Political Almanac 56
National Association of Latino Elected Officials (NALEO) 56, 57
National Black Caucus of State Legislators 56
National Conference of State Legislators (NCSL) 56
National Organization for Women (NOW) 27

Native American legislators, data on 56, 57
Native American men 56, 86; *see also* Native American legislators
Native American women 10, 54, 56, 32, 114; *see also* Native American legislators; women of color

ordinary least squares (OLS) regression coefficients 94–5, 104–5

per capita income 1, 26
political cultures: and geographical variation 15, 16, 23n35, 26, 34, 102n25; Individualistic 27, 38, 45n17; influence of 26, 28, 95, 104, 105, 106; Moralistic 26–8, 36, 38, 45n17, 87, 89, 93, 98, 102n25, 108–9; Traditionalistic 16, 27, 28, 38, 45n17, 87, 92, 93, 98, 103, 105, 106, 108–9, 113
political ideology: conservative 27, 38, 88, 92, 119; liberal 27, 28, 34, 36, 38–9, 89, 95, 96, 98, 104, 105, 106, 108–9
political parties: control model for 100–101n16; influence of 120; party affiliation 2; party control 105; party dominance 26; party organizations/structures 34, 120; recruitment for 2; strength of 110n2; *see also* Democratic Party; Republican Party
professionalized legislatures 27, 28–30, 32, 36, 39–40, 89, 95, 98, 104, 105, 106, 107–10, 113
Protestant religious denominations (conservative) 27

Index

race/ethnicity: and gender 29, 30, 33–4, 86, 103, 110, 113, 115, 121; impact of 2, 16, 17; *see also* ethnicity
racial gap 37
representation: descriptive 6, 19–20n12, 26, 98, 121; geographical variations in 11, 13–14, 15–16, 25–6; by legislators of color 33–5; state level 4–7; *see also* states, legislative representation in
Republican Party 2, 88, 100–101n16

sex-role expectations 119
Sharkansky's scale 87
single-member districts 98, 107
single-primary states 27
socioeconomic status 44–5n14, 96
states, legislative representation in: aggregate percentage summary (women) 10; bottom ten states (legislators of color) 63; bottom ten states (women) 60; demographics of 4–7; gender gap in 72–81; increase/decrease (legislators of color) 70–72; increase/decrease (women) 66–8; percentages of women in 8–9, 10, 11, 12; proportional representation (women) 12–13; ranking for gender gap, highest/lowest 77–80; regression coefficients for minority participation in 94–5, 104–5; top ten states (legislators of color) 62; top ten states (women) 59; variation in representation between 7–14; women as percentage of total 8–9; women of color in legislatures 36; *see also* representation

term limits 30–31, 32, 102n24

urbanization 26

variables: dependent 86–7; gender gap 72–81; historical patterns 64–8; independent 87–8, 98; states ranked as 58–64; regarding women in legislatures 37–42, 54–6; women compared to men 68–72
voters: attitudes of 1; African American 15; women and minorities 5, 20n13
voting districts: *see* multimember districts; single-member districts
Voting Rights Act (VRA, 1965) 15, 30, 32, 34, 116; influence of 35, 36, 40–41

white legislators 10; *see also* white men
white men: as incumbents 31; and politics 117; in single-member districts 41; *see also* men, and politics; white legislators
white women: ambition in 118–19; conditions favorable for 30, 108, 114; data on 112; election of 31; and the gender gap 103–4, 113, 116; and geographic variation 86, 113; historical trends for 64–8; hypotheses about 38–40; as legislators 33, 86–7; in multimember districts 41, 116; as officeholders 2–4; percentage in state legislatures 8–9, 10, 11, 12, 25, 61, 115; and politics 110, 117;

in pool of candidates 37–8; in state legislatures 90; variables influencing election of 37–42, 107; *see also* white legislators; women; women legislators

women: ambition in 25, 117–20; decline in legislative service of 24–5, 31; educated 27–8; election of 31, 27–42; growth in representation by 7, 54; historical trends for 64–8; percentage in state legislatures 8–9, 10, 11, 12; in politics 4, 5, 116–17; potential pool of candidates 27–8; predictors of state-level descriptive representation 109; professional 16, 27, 38 42, 87, 89–93, 95–8, 105–9, 111n5, 113; as representatives 6, 89, 112; in state legislatures 90; underrepresentation of explained 26–9; as voters 20n13; *see also* white women; women legislators; women of color

"women-friendly" districts 41, 53n79, 100–101n16, 110

women legislators: data on 56; hypotheses about 38–40; significance of 121; in variables between states 58–64; *see also* white women; women of color

women of color: ambition in 118–19; as candidates 35; compared to men of color 71–2; conditions favorable for 108; data on 57; defined 22n26; election of 31; gender gap and 10, 14, 103–4, 107, 113, 115; and geographic variation 86, 103, 112, 113; historical trends for 64–8, 68–72; hypotheses about 38–40; as legislators 2–4, 31–3, 36, 86–7, 121–2; in multimember districts 41, 116; percentage of in legislatures 86; percentage in state legislatures 8–9, 10, 11, 12, 25, 61; in pool of candidates 37–8; as representative term 57; variables influencing election of 37–42, 114; and variations in state legislature, 90; *see also* women; women legislators